# CHICKEN SCRATCH

Stories of Love, Risk, & Poultry

Kelly Chripczuk

Copyright © 2016 by Kelly Chripczuk.

Kelly Chripczuk
www.afieldofwildflowers.blogspot.com

Book Layout ©2013 BookDesignTemplates.com
Edited by Andi Cumbo-Floyd at andilit.com

Chicken Scratch/ Kelly Chripczuk -- 1st ed.
ISBN - 13: 978-1537170909
ISBN   10: 1537170902

*For my husband, always, and for our brood.*

*In loving memory of Cheeps*
*2014-2016*

*We're here to witness.*
*There's nothing else to do.*

– ANNIE DILLARD

# CONTENTS

# INTRODUCTION

I fell in love twice in the spring of 1998. Once at a diner seated across the table from a boy who read aloud his favorite lines from Jack Kerouac's *On the Road*. Then again in a basement classroom where I discovered the Psalms.

I was led to the basement classroom by our small Christian college's general education requirements. After completing a required Old Testament Survey class, I was now taking an upper level class on the Psalms. Having grown up in Christian churches, I was overly familiar with the books and letters of the New Testament, but the Hebrew Bible struck me as an entirely different beast. It was filled with stories – sto-

ries I either hadn't heard or paid much attention to in the past – and poetry.

Walking through the Psalms with my professor as a guide I discovered poems, prayers and songs that gave voice to the whole gamut of human experience. More familiar with the abstract theological arguments of the New Testament epistles, I was unprepared for the earthy, practicality of the Hebrew authors, the way they described God as molding humans from clay or visiting with Abraham outside of his tent on a hot day. The Old Testament revealed to me in a way I had yet to learn or had somehow forgotten that God shows up in common experiences. The Psalmists swept me off my feet with lines of praise, petition, and lament; their use of linguistic tools like metaphor, simile and repetition awoke me to the possibility of finding God in the world around us and using language to witness to the reality of that presence.

Seated on a curb beside the boy from the diner, biding time between classes, I tried to explain my discovery. "It's like the psalmists stood in the crossroads of life describing what they saw, giving witness to what is and where God is in it," I said. There in the clear sunlit spring, I envisioned the psalmists positioned at the intersection between heaven and earth, writing, singing and praying from the very center of their lives and thus proclaiming God's presence no

matter where they were. That spring the world felt full of possibility, full of God, by which I mean, full of love. I'm not sure what the boy with the Kerouac novel thought of my ramblings, but he seemed happy enough there beside me positioned between the green grass and the black of the road unwinding in front of us.

I fell in love twice that spring while the world bloomed green and fresh around me – in love with the boy beside me with his brown hair and kind brown eyes and in love with a vision of the world infused with the presence of God – every single thing endowed with meaning, purpose and revelation. I determined that year that I would study the Psalms in graduate school, become a scholar of the Hebrew Bible and teach others to fall in love with it as I did. I thought I was supposed to study the Psalms and I did, but what I discovered along the way is that I am in some way called to be like the psalmists were – to stand in the crossroads of life to witness to what is and where God is in it, to believe and declare that there's no arena of life in which God is not able to be known.

Fast forward 16 years and that boy with the brown eyes and I found ourselves searching for a house that would accommodate our family of six. By 2008, we

had welcomed two children – Sophia and Solomon – and had a comfortable family of four. Then, in 2011, we added an unexpected set of twin boys – Isaiah and Levi. We had outgrown our home and I was looking for more space, inside and out. My husband was looking for a place where we could have chickens.

Every house we looked at, and there were many, elicited the same question. "Do you think we could have chickens here?" Chickens had become a symbol for the way of life we sought, a life more spacious and rooted in nature than the one we had living in a small bungalow in town on $1/10^{th}$ of an acre of land. When we finally found our new home, one of the first things we did was drive to the local farm store to purchase five fluffy chicks. Those chickens represented a dream come true, and the dream unfolded and multiplied over two years and two sets of chicks who lived and died in varying numbers until the spring of 2016 when I became obsessed with the idea of getting more hens and selling eggs for profit.

That spring we'd lost one of our flock to an unknown, nighttime predator. We'd emerged from the house in the morning to find a trail of feathers and body parts leading across our yard. With that death, we were down to four hens, which meant three or four eggs a day if we were lucky, and I wanted more. I was convinced I could make a profit selling eggs along our

semi-rural road that runs through a little yuppie town known for fly fishing and its intersection with the Appalachian Trail. I pictured our health-conscious, upwardly-mobile neighbors lining up to buy fresh, free-range eggs as quickly as our hens could lay them. I decided we needed more chickens and we needed them now.

But, as is usually the case with compulsive decision-making, there was more to the story than the desire to establish a new source of income. The school year was drawing to a rapid end, summer's chaos loomed, and our youngest boys were turning five and entering kindergarten in the fall. I was approaching a major life transition as the shape of my mothering, which was a corner piece of my identity, was set to change drastically. After ten years of almost full-time mothering, my babies were leaving the nest. I wondered what I would do and, more importantly, who I would be in the face of so much open time and space. I felt the urge to pursue a life of writing and spiritual direction rooted in my life at home, but I was afraid to pursue it. I was afraid to fail and, more deeply, I was afraid of losing a new sense of self that had emerged after years of wrestling with my roles as a writer, a mother, and a minister of the gospel.

I wanted chickens, but on some semi-conscious level what I really wanted was something to wed me more

deeply to the life I already have. I wanted something to tie me to this place and to help me grow deep roots in the person I've become. I can't explain exactly why I thought a business selling eggs might do the trick, but it was worth a try.

This book started as a journal, a commitment to pay attention and write as often as I could during the first thirty days with our new flock. I wrote nearly every day from the first of May to the first of June, 2016. I paid attention to the way life with the birds intersected with my own life and family life. I watched the way I behaved with the birds and how I thought about them. I listened to my life and discovered the questions I would have to answer and decisions I needed to make to be able to embrace a life I love. Not all of my writings made the cut and much in the form of details and explanations was added later.

I watched the chickens, watched myself and listened for the nudge of God in the intersections of my life. And while I don't often write directly about God in the pages that follow, I'm convinced that the presence of love, grace and joy on these pages means God is here just as clearly as God is there in the longings, confessions, hopes and angst of the Psalms. I'm still in love with that brown-eyed boy, and this past spring

the world was again blooming fresh and green around us. Sleeping creation woke from its winter slumber and I stood for a while at the crossroads of love and risk where heaven and earth meet, waiting, watching and giving witness.

# 1   HAPPY BIRTHDAY TO ME

We arrived at the stranger's farm around nine o'clock on the morning of my 39th birthday. I had found the flock on Craigslist - 16 laying hens, plus two baby Polish hens for $50. I texted my husband at work with the good news and we emailed immediately. "We'll take them!" we wrote. But the owner was hesitant at best.

"They're pets," she wrote. "These girls are loved." She asked us to send pictures of our yard and coop. "Do you have chickens?" she asked. "I let them out at seven every morning and they eat from my hand," she added.

We exchanged over a dozen emails as she hemmed and hawed over our chicken rearing qualifications. It seemed unlikely we would make the cut. Frustrated, my husband and I joked that tax returns and personal references might be next on her list of demands. By mid-week, we got a frantic email explaining that her dog was having a medical crisis and then her emails stopped. We waited. Finally, toward the end of the week I sent one final inquiry, was she still interested in selling the birds?

"Yes," she replied, with a caveat – the flock was now down to 14 hens as a fox had been plucking them off one-by-one. By the end of the week the flock dwindled further to ten adults and two babies, but they were ours if we wanted them. Still, driving to her house Saturday morning, we worried she might withdraw her offer at the last minute, especially as we planned to jam her precious "pets" into recycled liquor boxes.

With the kids away at a friend's house, we were on a mission to collect the birds and get them settled in their new home before our children returned. The chickens were waiting for us, still cooped up tight from the night before. Normally, the owner let her hens out by seven am at the latest, so by the time we arrived they were impatient to start another day of free-ranging and foraging. They were indignant and then

furious when their owner cracked the door to the coop and started pulling them out one at a time.

We stuffed them into boxes marked "Smirnoff Ice" and "Captain Morgan's," small boxes we picked up free from the back room of the local liquor store. John had cut air holes into the boxes, slicing with his utility knife in the passenger seat as I drove us across town to the distant farm.

It took four of us, the owner and her husband and my husband and I, working together to wrangle the flapping, squawking birds into our improvised travel containers. The owner would pass me a chicken, which I battled into a box, then my husband closed the lid, folding the flaps one under the other to try to prevent escape. This we would need to repeat for each and every bird.

We were about half-way through packing up the hens when the trashing and squawking of the already boxed birds caused their boxes to collapse. One-by-one the birds toppled their way to escape and scattered across their owner's green grass. Alarmed, we chased and dove after them. If they spread into the fields and woods beyond the house, we wouldn't see them all again before evening when they came home to roost. While John and I hesitated, the birds' owner unceremoniously grabbed two by their tail feathers and crammed them into a waiting box. My husband and I,

who had handled the birds gingerly up until then, exchanged a surprised look. Maybe we didn't need to be quite as gentle with her "pets" as we thought.

In the end, we corralled five birds in boxes and five in a large dog crate the owner let us borrow. The two baby Polish hens traveled in their own small cage. The adult birds quieted as soon as we started driving, but the babies cried a steady stream of peeps. With the back seats out, we had a van packed to the gills with chickens and it smelled like it too, but that didn't stop us from stopping at a few yard sales on the way home.

Back at our house, we grabbed a quick lunch and went to ready the new coop. Our older hens live in a small mobile coop, built just big enough to house about five hens, so we needed a separate coop for the new flock, but couldn't afford to build one. While we had been looking for hens, we asked around among friends and looked online for unwanted outbuildings or playhouses we might adapt. But we found the birds before we found a coop, which led to the need to improvise. Thankfully, our sprawling garage offered a workable solution. A small room in the back, with a door opening to the garage and another to the back yard, seemed like a perfect fit. Cement floors meant easy cleaning, and windows would make it a sunny place for the birds to winter.

We scattered straw across the floor, opened the window for ventilation, and set up roosting bars and the all-important nesting boxes. Then, we unpacked the girls, unloading all of the boxes and crates into the coop and opening them one-by-one. The hens settled in quickly. Finding the nesting boxes, they piled in two and three at a time, eager to lay their eggs for the day.

Our old coop's small dimensions had kept us separated from our older flock's coop life, but the new coop allowed room for us to stand inside. After clearing away the boxes, John and I hung around watching and listening as the hens explored and nestled into the nesting boxes. Positioned just inside the door I heard a low purring noise, almost like a growl, coming from one of the laying birds. She seemed to be singing, quietly, over her nest. I was mesmerized with joy and wonder.

Eventually, we shut the door and went to tend to the adorable Polish hens. Although they come in a variety of colors, Polish hens are distinguished from other breeds by a huge pompom of feathers on top of their head. These two were a lacey gray and black and sported an outlandish white bouffant of feathers on their heads. Adorable. Timid and skittish, they huddled together emitting little peeps and high-pitched honking sounds. About twelve weeks old, they were

scarcely teenagers and had been kept separate from the older hens to avoid the sometimes brutal bullying that accompanies introduction to a flock. Since the new flock was already under stress from transition, we planned to integrate the Polish hens with our old flock and tucked them, cage and all, into the old coop's run.

In the afternoon the kids came home and met their newest pets. Delighted, they stood in the new coop gathering eggs, marveling at the colors of the new birds and assigning names. The moment my oldest son, Solomon, laid eyes on one of the Polish hens, he shouted loud enough for the whole neighborhood to hear, "That one's mine! I love it with all my heart!"

The following day, a Sunday, I had second thoughts. I was overwhelmed by the sheer number of birds and their needs. How could I possibly keep up with it all? But even as I wondered, I remembered talking with my husband the day before as we drove home with the van full of smelly birds. We talked about the pets we've accumulated since moving to this old farm – the cats, the dog, and now, the hens.

"I really enjoy animals," I had said, as though it might come as a surprise.

"Yeah," he said, "I noticed."

Groping for words, for understanding of my own dawning awareness, I added, "They help me see different ways of being." I told him how I watched our tomcat, Blackie, and the dog, Coco, this spring. When the weather turned warm for a few unexpected days in early March, I felt a sudden pressure to be outside, to be active in the yard taking full advantage of the long-awaited weather. But after being trapped in the house all winter, I didn't have the faintest idea what to do in the yard and the twins were also at a loss. Despite two acres of green grass, trees to climb and a rope swing swaying, they clamored around my feet whining and clinging, looking to me for direction whenever we ventured out. We had forgotten how to be outside.

Perplexed, I started watching the cat and the dog. I noticed how they sauntered out the back door sniffing the air and pausing every couple of steps. They laid in the sun, rolled in the grass. They stretched their way slowly into the yard, leisurely shedding winter and opening, as the whole world does in spring, toward a new season. Watching them, I found freedom to do the same.

The Sunday after we bought the birds, I arrived at church just in time to hear the tail end of the sermon. The final slide on the big projector's screen was about birds and joy, about the songs birds sing and the ones we sing too. It felt like a happy coincidence. The

morning after the birthday flock arrived, I stood with my church family singing *Joy to the World*, repeating the last line in the last verse about the wonders of God's love over and over again. I can't say exactly what wonders the hymn's author had in mind, but I'm almost certain a hen singing over her nest counts as one of them.

# 2 DELIBERATE FALTERING

I forgot. Or maybe I didn't realize.

Either way, though, I didn't take into account the extra work 12 more chickens would add. Extra poop, extra hay, extra cleaning inside the house and out. Every day the Polish hens dump their water, once in the morning and once at night. Every day they need to be fed, twice a day. Then, they must be placed in the coop with the older hens and kept under a watchful eye in case bullying breaks out – which it always does. At night they must be captured and tucked away again in their solitary cage.

The ten grown hens, cooped until they realize this is where they live, must be fed and watered. Foamy mounds of poop must be scraped off of the lids of the nesting boxes where they roost at night. Eggs must be gathered, frequently, to keep them from being accidentally knocked out of the nest or eaten. Egg-eating hens are counter-productive to an egg business' bottom line, and the behavior must be firmly discouraged. One of the best ways to dissuade egg-eaters is to cut off their supply, and since I've now caught one or two hens in the act, I'm gathering eggs as often as possible. Also, eggs sales have been disappointingly slow and our refrigerator is beginning to overflow with filled egg cartons.

It turns out that the idea of 12 chickens is different than the reality of 12 chickens, and the idea of selling eggs is easier and more lucrative than the reality. It's possible this new investment won't be as successful as I had hoped it would.

I told my counselor about the chickens at the end of my appointment this week. I was already standing and halfway to the door to leave when I told her about the birds. Summing things up, I said, "I don't know how it's going to go, but I guess that's ok. It's an adventure."

"Really?" she said, "Twelve chickens? That's a lot! Where do you get 12 chickens? Will you sell the eggs?"

I explained the origins of our flock, the fact that they were a birthday present, of sorts, to myself, and that, yes, we would be selling eggs. Then, feeling flustered by her astonishment, I rapidly backpedaled on my plan. "We can always turn around and sell them for twice what we bought them for," I said. This is the kind of thing I say to hide my own uncertainty. Inside, I worry about failure; outside, I offer sound reasoning as to why it's a certain success. I'm not always sure who I'm trying hardest to convince, my audience or myself.

"Hey, it sounds like fun," she replied, "and it's no big deal if it doesn't work out."

Then, I turned awkwardly serious, more serious than the brief exchange demanded. "I know that," I said, "but it's one thing to know it's ok to fail and another to experience failure. I need to create chances to fail, so I can feel it all the way down, not just know it in my head."

She looked surprised at my earnest proclamation. Smiling, she said, "I'm looking forward to hearing chicken stories."

The next day I stood in the kitchen as the older kids arrived home from school. As I listened for the sound of the bus chugging over the hill, something outside the window caught my eye. Turning, I saw a cluster of red and brown birds gathered around a puddle in the driveway. It took me a second to comprehend what I was seeing. Then it hit me – the new hens were out, free, in the driveway, all ten of them. This was not supposed to be. If we didn't catch them quickly, they were likely to wander off and get lost or worse. Just then, Sophia popped in the door.

"You know the new chickens are out, right?" she asked.

"No. Well, yes, but they're not supposed to be out," I said. Solomon darted in next, followed by Isaiah and Levi, and everyone whirled and clamored around me until I shouted above the chaos, "The chickens! We need to get the chickens!"

It was a battle cry, and all five of us rushed out to the driveway, where the chickens stood casually drinking, unperturbed by their own shocking prison break. The first three or four were easy to catch. I tucked them two-at-a-time under my arms and marched them back to the coop, taking care to latch the door securely behind me. But the stragglers sensed their impending capture and scattered, running frantically around the house and yard.

Then, the hunt began in earnest. The kids and I gave chase while shouting unhelpful advice at whoever was closest to a fleeing bird. "Get it! Go! Grab her!" we cried. Chickens are fast and low to the ground, which makes them hard for an adult to nab. Picture chasing a dollar bill across the beach on a windy day; every time you bend to grab, it flies just out of reach. They also used our overgrown shrubs to their advantage. Thankfully, though, chickens aren't terribly smart and, once we realized the key to capture lay in brains, not brawn, the playing field tilted to our advantage. Soon we were tag-teaming the hens, one or two kids corralling them into a tight corner, then a third running in for the catch.

Eventually, they were all back inside. I counted twice to be sure. No hens died, none were lost. We even had a little fun. Bobbing and weaving through the yard, I slowly shed my initial panic and alarm. The stakes are never as high as I fear them to be. I was not alone and nothing was lost. The jury may still be out on this whole adventure, whether it will be a failure or success, but I'm claiming today as a win.

# 3   COOPED UP

We kept the birthday flock locked in their coop for almost a week. Their previous owner had allowed them to free-range, wandering open fields at-will during the day, and we planned to do the same. But, for now, they needed to stay inside long enough to develop a new sense of home. Otherwise, they're likely to wander off and end up lost or dead. "Keep them cooped for two weeks, at least," a friend recommended. "Three, even," another added.

So we shut them into the 10x20 coop with nesting boxes, roosting bars, and food and water aplenty. I

visited them three or four times a day, checking for eggs, changing water, adding food and offering treats like stale cereal and popcorn. "Peep, peep," I said as I opened the door, teaching them the call we use with the old flock and to associate the sight and sound of my arrival with reward.

For the first several days, the hens settled happily, overcoming the stress of transition and relaxing in the new, clean environment. I began to think that maybe, by the end of the first week, we could let them out into the sunlit yard for some fresh air and green grass if the kids and I kept a close watch. But towards the end of the week, rain descended for days on end, and plans to enjoy the yard while chickens wandered were scrapped.

Days of confinement passed, and the daily egg count dropped dramatically. The hens broke out and scattered in the driveway and yard once and then again when we failed to securely latch the coop door. By day six, they were looking pretty desperate. The mood in the coop was tense and agitated. Now whenever I approached the door one bird, always the same one, flew up and hurled herself at the window. Although reason told me she was only trying to escape, it felt like she was aiming for my face. On purpose. Soon, whenever I visited with food and water or to gather eggs, fear rose in my chest. My body tensed,

movements slowed, I treated them like prisoners on lock-down, not daring to expose my back for fear of a surprise attack. In my mind, they were a teaming mob ready to turn on me with a moment's notice. Would the kids return from school one day to find the chickens wandering free and their mother trampled in the garage, the victim of a chicken stampede? I hoped not.

One day, as I again shut the door in their pleading faces, it dawned on me – they were "cooped up." I heard the familiar phrase ring in my mind with new clarity and depth as words used to convey an idea took on flesh and blood, wing and talon, right in front of my eyes. I thought then of the endless stream of snow days in winter, the rainy days and weeks of summer when the kids and I are trapped together at home for long stretches of time. At first, the cloistering seems a welcome respite from daily demands, but then as the days linger and stretch out before us with no certain end in sight, the atmosphere slowly changes. The welcome closeness turns stifling. Small fights and bickering turn to battles as the lovely sense of togetherness gives way to a desperate need for space and time apart. In those times, we too feel cooped up.

These linguistic awakenings are one of my favorite things about doing something new. Tending the chickens, I hear old words and phrases anew and discover dimensions of meaning I never knew existed. Language that was flat and familiar becomes three-dimensional, one might even say incarnational, fleshed-out with the texture of flesh and bone, feather and beak.

In the two years we've owned chickens, I've had the opportunity to observe broody hens and faced the challenge of wrestling eggs from under their wide, warm breasts. A broody hen is determined and focused. As eggs accumulate in the nest, she enters an almost trance-like state where she sits, staring, for hours on end, leaving only once a day for a bit of food and water. Once satisfied, she stops laying new eggs, output ceases as she focuses all her attention on sitting on the eggs. This continues for weeks, regardless of whether there are actually eggs to sit on and whether those eggs are fertilized. By the end of a period of brooding, a hen is thin and worn, her chest feathers sacrificed to the nest.

Observing this, the word "brooding" flashes brighter and richer in my mind. Now, I see how brooding often involves needless worry, a focus of attention that's unfruitful and distracts us from real productivity. Prolonged brooding may leave us worn out and

sick, or it may be a necessary sacrifice in the work of bringing forth new life.

Watching the hens "hunt and peck" for grain and bugs in the grass, jabbing their pointy beaks here then there, I realize it is exactly the same pause, lunge, repeat method new typists employ on an unfamiliar keyboard. Noticing their scattered footprints in the dirt, a tangle of divots and lines wreaking havoc on landscaping, I know with certainty how accurate it is to describe my oldest boy's terrible handwriting as "chicken scratch," the way his letters march haphazardly across the page, tilting and toppling over each other, his eraser tearing holes in the paper where I force him to try again and again to write legibly.

Every one of these linguistic awakenings brings a ping of delight to my writer's heart. "Ah-ha!," I think, "so *that's* what we mean." This is what I love about doing new things. If a new experience is arousing enough, off-kiltering enough, then it can force us to wake up, to pay better attention to the world around us. An attentive mind is an open mind, ready for whatever comes its way, and in the midst of learning a new trick or trade, one is often blessed with happy little bonuses like the linguistic awakenings I love. The material world is wedded to the immaterial and the gift of language allows us to span the gap between the two. Words, strung like beads on a nearly invisi-

ble thread, connect experiences and ideas into a cluster of communicable meaning. This, for me, is a source of endless joy and delight.

Near the end of the week, my husband pulled into the driveway with a large roll of thin plastic netting tucked into the cab of his red pickup truck. The next day, when the sun finally returned, we rolled it out and staked it into three sides of a square, using the garage wall with the coop's exterior door as the fourth side.

Now, our girls had a run, and we were relieved to give them the luxury of grass between their toes and sunshine on their fluffy backs. The six of us gathered around in eager anticipation to open the door, but the hens didn't rush out like we thought they might. Filled with caution, they paused at the door, peering sideways through orange eyes. Slowly, eventually, all ten found their way into the yard. Soon, they were tearing into the grass with voracious appetites, exploring the wood pile, and looking for ways to escape their new confinement. I stood in the run with them watching and waiting to see what I might discover next.

# 4 LIFE AND DEATH

At the end of my appointment this week, my counselor asked about the chickens. "What will you do when they," here she paused and lowered her voice, ". . . stop laying?"

A hen's egg production declines rapidly after two or three years, and I get this question a lot, the pause and lowered voice acknowledging that talk of death – even the death of a chicken – is inherently taboo in our culture. Some, like my counselor, respond to my blank look by following the initial question with a second more direct inquiry involving hand gestures. "Will you . . . ," she asked, swinging her hand across

her throat and simultaneously tilting her head to one side. I'm not sure what kind of gruesome act she was trying to mime – decapitation or worse – but her point was clear.

Usually I shrug my shoulders and raise my eyebrows in response. "I don't know," I say. Lately I add the enigmatic phrase, "Things happen to chickens," placing emphasis on the word *things*. In this way, I guess, chickens are a bit like outdoor cats. We went through a lot of cats when I was a kid, and I used to entertain my friends with stories of their unfortunate deaths and near-death experiences. I loved those cats, but I understood enjoying the life of a pet also meant enduring its death. Similarly, my kids already have and will likely continue to go through a lot of chickens, and I believe they'll have some good stories to tell.

Our first poultry death was not accidental. We got our first set of five chicks two years ago from a local farm supply store. Each ball of fluff was hand-picked from several large metal feeding troughs filled with birds separated by breed. They were named before we even got home. Our kids adored those birds, carrying them through the house singing and talking to them, holding them up to the windows to "see" the great outdoors. Over time, as we shuffled the birds from brooder to hand-built coop, our oldest son developed a deep bond with his bird, a beautiful Rhode Island Red

named Cinnamon. In time, though, Cinnamon grew from a sweet ball of reddish-brown fluff into a wily and fierce rooster. We hadn't planned to have a rooster and didn't know what the neighbors might think of the noise, but we didn't mind his crowing. After all, he was Solomon's favorite.

But as he grew, Cinnamon became territorial about his hens and coop and our son was nipped and spurred several times when trying to care for them. Each time Solomon came to me crying from his injuries, I felt my heart harden a little toward the rooster. Cinnamon also developed a horny streak a mile wide. Worn out by his appetites, the four hens took to hiding in the coop whenever they could. By fall, we'd had enough. One day, a dear friend and veteran chicken owner stopped by with a cat carrier, and we unceremoniously loaded Cinnamon inside. It was not a dignified exit. We told the kids he was going to be rehomed, but back at her house, she had her son dispatch him with an axe.

The four hens survived the winter, but one day in the spring I walked out to the yard to find one stretched out dead in the run. It looked like she just keeled over in the middle of an otherwise uneventful day. I called my husband at work because, despite being a fully liberated woman in many areas of life, I still firmly believe dead pets fall into the category of

"men's work." "We have a dead chicken," I reported. John said I should move the bird and put in our trash bin to avoid the possible spread of disease. Instead, I left the poor hen where she lay and went on with my day, avoiding looking in the general direction of the chicken coop. I doubt this surprised him in the least.

That night, John poked around in the coop and run, investigating. There was no sign of foul play – it appeared illness was at fault. In particular, there seemed to be a lot of diarrhea. It turns out that many chicken illnesses involve diarrhea. This isn't some-thing they tell you when you pick out those cute little balls of fluff. Worried, we kept an eye on the rest of the flock and, sure enough, a day or two later a second hen grew lethargic and stopped laying. John brought her into the house early one morning before leaving for work. Donning gloves, he gently checked her backside for signs of a stuck egg or prolapse, but it was too late, she died right there in his hands.

We were disappointed to lose those two hens after seeing them through a long, cold winter and worried we might also lose the remaining two. But the virus passed, and a few weeks later, we drove to the farm store again and added three new babies to the flock. We kept those five chickens – two old and three new – all through the following summer, fall, and winter. Then this spring, when I was already dreaming of more

birds and more eggs, we suffered another loss. I blamed my husband for the death, and he blamed the fluffy pine tree in our yard.

The previous summer, the hens had developed the habit of roosting overnight in a small pine tree that we call "the Christmas tree." Wide and dense, the tree lures both children and chickens to its branches. Once settled for the night, it was nearly impossible to coax the hens out of the tree and into the coop. For a long time, John struggled through the branches every night, plucking them one-by-one from the tree like sleepy, feathered fruit. Eventually, he abandoned the nightly collection and accepted the habits of our feral chickens who slept in the tree and, occasionally, laid eggs under it.

During the winter, we kept them penned in the co-op for safety and warmth and hoped they'd forget about their nights of wild freedom in the boughs of the Christmas tree. But in the spring, they reverted back to sleeping in the pine tree. We weren't pleased, but in chicken farming, as in life, one must eventually come to accept that there's only so much you can control.

Unfortunately, one morning in early spring, John discovered a trail of blonde feathers spread across the yard. Following the path, he found a string of intestines stretched out in the green grass. I awoke a few

hours later to a note on the kitchen counter. "T3 died," was all it said. That left just one hen remaining from our original flock of five. Maybe something climbed into the tree and grabbed her or maybe she fell out of the tree in her sleep and was taken for a hawk's easy prey. Regardless, I blamed John for not cooping them at night, and he blamed the Christmas tree for providing convenient and tempting shelter. He said we should cut down the tree; I said we needed more hens.

I've read a lot of chicken farming books over the last two years. Most are coffee-table style books aimed at exploiting an upwardly-mobile, middle class attraction to a glorified and highly-sanitized version of farm life. These artful books cover the pleasant topics of breed choices, housing and the joys of consuming fresh eggs.

Strikingly absent, though, are any significant discussions of common chicken farming pitfalls like birds dying of diarrhea and other illnesses and treating for common mites, stuck eggs, and other ailments like a particularly nasty condition called "pasty butt." Nothing I've read directly addresses the hairy question of what to do when your fluffy chick turns out to be a rooster – which is a fairly common occurrence – or how to explain to your children why your hen-turned-rooster keeps actually injuring the hens in his lusty

pursuit of sexual expression. Even fewer books broach the awkward question of, "What will you do when . . . ?"

One result of our hands-on education in the real texture of life and death as it pertains to poultry is that we've all become less attached. The kids named the second batch of chicks, but I still can't tell who's who and the new flock is mostly a blur of nameless faces, save for a few odd birds whose appearance or behavior marks them as unique. I'd like to think this isn't a callousness but more a simple acceptance of the way life and death, sickness and health, are inter-twined in the tapestry of life. It's never fun to lose a bird, and we do everything we can to avoid inflicting needless suffering, but something about this new-found openness to death and the "what will you do" questions it raises seems remarkably true and good. Also, it makes for some darn good story telling.

# 5 LOVE LEADS

I woke on Mother's Day to a bouquet of cards, crafts, and kisses. Then, I showered, dressed, and climbed into my husband's old, red pickup truck and drove to church to preach a sermon about chickens. I showed a great deal of restraint by not carting a chicken or two along with me to serve as a visual aid. I had considered it, mid-week, but ideas like that often, thankfully, lose steam as the week progresses. By the time Sunday rolled around, I opted to leave my new feathered friends at home.

I planned to speak on Jesus' lament over Jerusalem in Luke 13:34, "Jerusalem, Jerusalem, the city that

kills the prophets and stones those who are sent to it! How often have I desired to gather your children together as a hen gathers her brood under her wings." It seemed like the perfect passage for me, complete with a female image of God's love and a reference to chickens, which made my non-stop obsession with the new flock technically count as sermon prep.

I was in love with chickens, and that love, that natural curiosity and awe, offered fertile soil for reflecting on the love of God as I tried to comprehend the meaning of Jesus' words. This is how I approach both writing and preaching. This is why one month I preach a sermon on chickens, and the next it's an avocado tree grown from a seed rescued from the compost bin. Another time I may speak or write about the Zinnias dancing in my flower garden or a the images found in a favorite children's book. I always look for a point of connection between myself and the world that somehow elucidates the connections between myself and the word. Whenever I fall in love with something, someone, I find that love, like an invisible thread, leads me back to God. The same can be said for any range of strong emotions – including the darker emotions like anger or hate or fear – these too can lead us back to God if we wrestle long and hard, but I find the road of love makes for a much more enjoyable journey and try to walk it as often as I can.

I'm not a chicken, not a hen, but I am a mother, and I do know what it feels like to gather my children close. So other than obvious observations of the hens, I spent time that week reflecting on the feeling of holding the ones you love close. I've never been a touchy person, not a hugger, not one to reach out and touch you on the arm while we talk. I'm more of a "give me my own space" kinda gal. But love has a habit of asking us for things we either don't want or don't have to give, and so in loving well, we're changed.

That Sunday morning during my Mother's Day sermon, I told the church about a class John and I had taken when we found out we were expecting twins. We already had two children, so we were familiar with child birth and infant care, but the impending arrival of twins had thrown us for a loop. So we went back to school, driving to the hospital on weeknights to sit in an impersonal room with strangers who also found themselves in the shocking situation of expecting multiples. What we really needed was time and space to wrap our heads around the impending doom of caring for two infants at once. Mostly, we sat and listened through a haze of thinly-veiled shock.

I'll always remember, though, a point at which the teacher – a mother of five including a set of twins – sat on the floor with her legs crossed to explain how she managed to nurse both babies at once. After demon-

strating several possible breastfeeding holds, she mo-
tioned toward the circle formed by her folded legs.
"My kids call this my nest," she said, "and they all
pile in as often as they can." I can't say for sure what
I thought at the time, but I imagine I was something
close to horrified at the thought of so many little people climbing, lounging, and feeding on me.

But the babies came, as they do, and my body
learned to make room on the outside as it had on the
inside. Or maybe it would be more accurate to say
that love made room. I learned to feed and burp two
babies at once, how to juggle one on each knee while
still listening attentively to an older child's dilemma. I
told my congregation, in my Mother's Day sermon,
about the difference between holding two babies and
one. Holding one child, your arms close in tight in
front of you, but with two, you're forced to sit up and
expand your chest, stretching your arms like wings to
encircle both. What I noticed, with time, was how
that holding opened me physically and emotionally
and changed me from a not-so-touchy person to a
woman who loves to feel the weight of a child pressed
into her lap.

Now my twins are growing just as their older siblings have and the moments they spend in my "nest"
are more fleeting every day. Now, I relish the morn-
ings when they stumble sleepily to my lap and the

times when while watching a movie together, they re-flexively back up to where I sit on the couch knowing, without even asking, that I will lift them into my lap. These days, I told the church, I feel the emptiness of my arms, the longing for the weight of my children pressed against me. "This," I said, "is what Jesus is saying about God. This is how God feels, this longing, this love, this desire to gather us in."

A chicken's love for her chicks is fierce; a mother's love for her children is fierce; and God's love for us is fierce, too.

After church, Sophia and I rode home side-by-side in the pickup truck and shared a few minutes alone before John arrived with the van full of boys. When we got home, we let the new hens out into the run and collected a couple of eggs; then, we ran inside together to get started on lunch. My daughter was happy and bright, carrying a clutch of eggs in her up-turned shirt. "This is so fun," she said, striding into the house, "our little chicken farm."

I popped fish sticks and french-fries into the oven then sat outside in the sun watching the new hens enjoying the run. This was one of the Polish hens' first days out foraging alongside of the adult hens. The sky was blue with little puffy clouds carried along on a

happy breeze. As I watched, the smaller Polish hen ran a few steps with her wings open then was surprised by a gust of wind that lifted her a foot or so off the ground. Startled, she scurried away, and I laughed at her accidental discovery of flight.

That night, I went out to check on the Polish hens again. The older hens had bullied them some throughout the day, as is to be expected when integrating new birds into an established flock, but nothing serious. I wondered if it might be ok to let them roost with the older hens at night. Peering through the window in the coop door, I saw the pair of them perched side-by-side on a roosting bar, like lovers tucked in together for the night. Their heads drooped in exhaustion after a long day of exercise and exploration. They were adorable, and I ran inside to call the kids out to witness the nearly unbearable cuteness. "Come see where the Polish hens are," I told Sophia. "It's so cute. They're roosting right next to each other."

"I know," she said, "I put them there." I savored the image of her mothering those bitty-birds, lifting them and gently setting them down beside each other.

Sometimes, I worry I'm not teaching my kids enough about the Bible. We have yet to memorize Bible verses. We don't do devotionals morning, noon, or night. Maybe as the kids grow older that area of

our life will improve. But for now, I know I'm giving my kids plenty of opportunities to love, and I believe love changes us, grows us, in ways we cannot foresee or even, sometimes understand. I trust that love is shaping my little flock just as it is shaping me.

# 6   THE GIFT OF GATHERING

After dropping Isaiah and Levi off at preschool, I pulled into our driveway to find four chickens had escaped from the run. Two were roaming the neighbor's yard and two more meandered along our side of the fence. I sighed and parked. Getting out, I threw my purse onto the roof of the van and followed the fence line into the back yard.

The first two birds were easily caught, one in each hand, and I tossed them back over the plastic netting into the outdoor run. Wings flapping, they landed and resumed their hunting and pecking unperturbed. Then, I scanned the yard, front and back, looking for

the other escapees. That's when I noticed our neighbor, a woman in her seventies who runs a Montessori preschool next door. Perched on top of high-heel wedges, her long, white hair swayed as she leaned out the door of the small preschool classroom. Several children leaned with her, staring at me while my hen pecked its way around her yard. "Your chicken's over here," she called.

"I know," I said. "I've got some to catch over here; then, I'll be over."

My audience disappeared back inside the school, and I turned my attention to a medium-sized brown hen nick-named the Lone Ranger because of a dark, mask-like marking across her face. She had wandered back into our yard, and I decided to catch her first before crossing into the neighbor's yard to hunt the fourth and final fugitive. Expecting a chase, I ran inside to the kitchen and filled a zip-lock bag with random scraps of food – slices of red pepper from dinner the night before and a left-over waffle from breakfast plus two handfuls of old fashioned oats.

Then, I headed back outside through the laundry room, the mud room, across the driveway, past the van, and into the back yard. I threw oats into the run where the captive birds swarmed, pecking and fighting over the treat. The scuttle for food drew the Lone Ranger's attention, and she ambled away from the

neighbor's fence and closer to the netting. As she approached, I bent and lunged to grab her, then tossed more food, and bent and lunged again. Every time, though, she shuffled just out of reach.

"Feeding the chickens?" I heard my neighbor's voice call from across the fence. She and her students were now at the back door of the preschool. They leaned out the door again, watching my clumsy display. My cheeks burned – few things are quite as humiliating as being outmaneuvered by a chicken in front of an unintended audience. "Oh, she has a lot of birds," she said commenting, I suppose, to the children gathered around her legs.

"Trying to catch this one here," I called, "then I'll be over for the other."

"You should climb the fence," she suggested.

I have, in the past, climbed the fence. Until recently, an old Bluetick Coonhound roamed the neighbor's yard, and I was quick to leap the chest-high fence to rescue chickens and cats from his sights. It was always a touch-and-go endeavor. My shoes could never find traction in the chain links and the whole fence wobbled and shook beneath me as I straddled the top bar, shifting one leg then the other over the top.

This past winter, all six of us climbed over to go sledding on the neighbor's hill. I went first, planning to catch the kids as John tossed them over, but I lost

my balance halfway through and flipped over backward off of the fence, landing flat on my back. The
solid landing stunned me, and everything was quiet for
a few seconds as my family waited to see if I was ok.
Then, I started laughing, and they all joined in, relieved. That day, a good three or four feet of snow
saved me from real harm, but I still remembered the
impact of my landing. There wasn't any snow to
break a fall now. No, I wouldn't be climbing the fence
today, definitely not with a bevy of little eyes watching my middle-aged mount and dismount.

"I think I'm getting a little old for that," I called
back. "I'll walk around."

I gave up on catching the Lone Ranger and walked
out to the road with my bag of treats in hand, ready
to confront the chicken in my neighbor's yard. I
marched up the road, down the neighbor's driveway,
through the gate and into the school yard. There, I
found our most frequent escapee, Bleach Blonde, a
buff-colored girl with a patch of white feathers in the
middle of her back.

"Peep, peep," I called. She was in the neighbor's
flowerbed, scratching up mulch with her feet, dancing
two steps forward then back to inspect the overturned
ground for insects to eat. With every scratch and
peck, she edged closer to a low wooden deck. It would
be almost impossible to catch her if she slipped under

it in her quest for food. "Peep, peep," I called again. With the cool shade of the deck looming, I needed to plan my moves carefully.

Until then, I had scattered oats right in front of me luring the hens close enough for me to make a grab at their fluffy backs. Every time, though, the birds saw my outstretched arms and scuttled away, leaving me grasping a handful of air rather than feathers. This time, though, I tried tossing the oats further to my left so the hen would need to walk past me, within grabbing distance, to eat them. Rather than facing me, she was now turned sideways and positioned just to my left. As she happily pecked at the oats, I bent and nabbed her on the first try.

My self-confidence restored, I tucked her under my arm, closed the neighbor's gate behind me and headed back down the driveway to the road and down the hill toward home. A truck drove by as I walked along with the chicken riding at my side and seeing the driver see me, I thought to myself, "This is where the phrase 'chicken lady' comes from."

Still in my yoga clothes, hair wild and frizzed, I placed the Bleach Blonde in the coop and headed toward the back yard for a final face-off with the Lone Ranger. I desperately hoped she hadn't wandered back into the neighbor's yard. As I walked along, I noticed a small opening at the corner of the run's rick-

ety plastic fencing, at the place where it butted up against the garage. Pausing to examine it more closely, I spied a well-worn path running through the grass on both sides of the hole - this was their escape hatch! I placed an old brick in the hole, then added a second brick and a piece of wood behind it. It was overkill, but I was so very ready to be done chasing chickens.

After blocking the hole, I walked into the back yard and discovered the Lone Ranger foraging near the compost bin. Sticking with what had worked before, I decided to get her attention by again throwing food over the plastic netting to the hens inside the run. The flurry of activity, the bright red peppers slices landing in the spring green grass, drew her like a magnet. Triumphant, I cornered her on the wood pile and tossed her into the run.

Once the fugitives were all behind bars again, I settled into my office to write for what was left of the twins' preschool hours. But as soon as my bottom hit the chair, I heard a thump at the door. The dog and I both looked and listened. I walked to the door and peered out the window. I didn't know what I would do if it was another chicken. I simply couldn't chase another chicken. Standing at the door, I heard a small peeping sound, but I couldn't tell where it was coming from.

Having learned from the morning's escapades that a little cleverness goes a long way when dealing with birds, I snuck out the back door and crept around to the front of the Little House. There on the doormat sat a little brown sparrow, panting. Her tiny beak was open, her eyes half-closed. Tentatively, I reached out and touched her, my fingers brushing the lightness of her back. She opened her eyes then closed them again. I assumed she'd flown into the window or door and was stunned from the impact. She would be fine but needed a moment to gather her wits. Thinking of our tomcat, who enjoys the occasional song bird snack, I decided to move the tiny bird.

Reaching out, I circled my fingers around her, gently teasing her delicate feet from their grip on the doormat. She didn't move a feather as I carried her a few steps away to our wild bird feeder and gingerly placed her on its ledge. Leaving her to rest, I returned again to my chair. When I checked later, she was gone.

That makes five birds I held in my hands that morning, five birds and two warm eggs while the day still stretched out ahead of me. I can't say for sure what those five birds – four gathered in frustration and one gently eased in tenderness – have to do with each other, except to say that one, perhaps, led to the other. They're connected, of course, by the silky fluff of

feathers and the light but weighty feel of life in my hands. Beyond that, though, I know that if I hadn't learned to handle a chicken, both in joy and frustration, I would not have believed I could reach out my hand and carry that sweet little songbird to safety. Somehow her need and my response shone a new light on the morning's trials.

# 7 COMMUNION

One morning, after Sophia and Solomon left for school, I left Isaiah and Levi inside the house flipping and flopping from couch to couch and headed out through a misty rain to check on the hens. Sneaking out the back door toward the garage, I welcomed the peace and quiet of the dripping sky as a necessary antidote to the morning's whirl of noise and demands.

Inside the coop, the Polish hens perched on a slender, curving tree branch that stretches from one side of the coop to the other. There they nestled together, sides touching. The rest of the hens milled around on

the straw-covered floor. The door to the run was open, but the hens lingered inside, avoiding the rain. I lifted the Polish hens down, one by one, and tucked them into the dog crate with water and food so they could eat and drink in peace.

Then, I shifted my attention to getting food and water for the rest of the flock. The big hens came with a large metal waterer that, once filled, slowly dispenses water into a shallow pool, providing continual access to clean water. It has a handle for hanging, so John rigged a rope and hung it in the new coop. The next day, we arrived to find the waterer empty and surrounded by a large swath of wet hay. Next we tried sitting it on the floor, but the chickens walked in it, pooped in it, and filled the shallow pool with so much hay there was nothing left to drink. That's when I decided chicken nipples might be the answer to our problem.

A chicken farming friend of mine posted something online once about chicken nipples. Unfamiliar with the basics of poultry husbandry, I wondered what in the world she was talking about. Then, I googled the phrase. A quick search assured me that chicken nipples aren't the actual nipples of chickens (do chickens even have nipples?), but rather, nipples *for* chickens. The small plastic and metal nozzles allow water to flow one drop at a time and work much like the small

mammal waterers you find in gerbil and hamster cages. Glue a few nipples into holes in the bottom of a plastic bucket, hang it by a string and, voila, you have a chicken waterer. Having made these for our old flock, we quickly rigged a new bucket, but the hens wanted nothing to do with it. They clearly preferred drinking from a pool or even an old puddle in the driveway when they could find one.

Today, I tried one more trick, finally pulling out a second waterer, called a Water Boy, given to us by the hen's former owner. The Water Boy is a clear plastic Tupperware type contraption that you fill with water and lay flat in the coop. A special sieve in the lid allows only a small amount of water to pool in the Water Boy's open mouth. The hens took to it happily, the minute I put it down, scooping water in their beaks then lifting their heads to swallow.

Next, I went to tend to the old flock. I refilled their food and water and surveyed the condition of the turf in their run. Our old hens live in a chicken tractor, another term that paints a picture nearly as misleading as the phrase "chicken nipple." A chicken tractor is an elevated coop surrounded by a small enclosed run, the whole thing rests on a set of wheels making it easily movable.

We pull the tractor through the yard, constantly exposing the hens to fresh grass which keeps them

from ruining any one patch of lawn and helps distribute their waste over a larger area. If you move a chicken tractor often enough, you never really need to clean the run, which was a huge selling point for me when we were researching and designing our first coop. Despite its wheels, our tractor's still crazy heavy and moving it is typically my husband's job. But this morning I managed to pull it forward a few feet, revealing fresh grass for the girls to work over with feet and beaks.

I checked on the chickens throughout the day, running out in the rain and drizzle to look for eggs, to let the baby hens out of the dog crate, and generally escape for a bit from the swarming of the twins inside.

In the afternoon, I sent the twins to their room for quiet time and went to my own room to unwind and do a little writing. Seated on my bed with the laptop in hand, I heard voices in the yard. Getting up, I looked out of an upstairs window and spied an unfamiliar red vehicle parked in the driveway. I left the boys rollicking loudly in their room, jogged downstairs, and threw open the back door. A couple from church stood in the rain near the chicken tractor. The wife held an empty egg crate in one hand and cash in the other, and I assumed they were here to buy eggs.

"We're peeking at your chickens," Jeannie said, leaning toward the coop with a smile. Jeannie and her

husband, Duane, have been in and out of our lives for over ten years. Close to retirement age, they don't have children of their own, and Jeannie loves to stop by from time to time with gifts for our kids. Once, when we still lived at our old house in town, Jeannie arrived with an enormous brown teddy bear, bigger than our oldest child at the time. The bear, dubbed Big Bear, joined my daughter's sleeping zoo before being passed on to her younger siblings. Big Bear, much wilted now, still floats around the house from room to room finding use alternately as a toy, a pillow, or a lovey. Duane and I both teach as adjuncts at local colleges and have served on a church board together, so despite an age difference we do have a good bit in common.

But I feel an intuitive connection with Jeannie. Jeannie grew up in poverty, the oldest daughter in a family of many kids. She speaks her mind freely, and often, and yet she's one of the most unintimidating people I know. Jeannie is the kind of person it would be easy to overlook unless you're listening for things beyond the surface like love, compassion, and kindness.

I walked out to join them in the rain, eager to share my birds with an interested audience. Jeannie had enjoyed my chicken sermon at church and was stopping by now to meet the girls for herself. "Did

John build this?" Duane asked, referring to the tractor.

"Yep." I said. "He built it, and I painted it." The chicken tractor was one of the first big projects we tackled after moving to our new old farm house. There were walls to paint, floors to sand, and a significant shower situation to amend inside of our house, but instead of tackling such practical demands, we worked outside on the driveway building the a-frame coop with its bright silver metal roof. John designed it himself, and I painted it in shades of raspberry and eggplant with lime green accents to add a little kick. The list of things we could've been doing was long, but the chicken tractor represented a dream come true and served as a stake in the ground regarding the kind of life we hoped to live in our new place.

"Do they all live in there?" Duane asked, peering at the small coop.

"No," I said, "our four older hens live there; the new chickens are in the garage. Do you want to see them?"

I led them to the garage, and we gathered outside the door to the coop, peering in through the window. "Look at them!" Jeannie gasped, leaning close to the glass for a better view. The door to the run was open, but most of the hens were inside.

"How many do you have?" Duane asked.

"Ten adults and the two baby Polish hens," I said.

"I like chickens," Jeannie said with emphasis. Then she handed the egg cartons to Duane. "I want to go in and talk to them," she said, opening the door.

"Watch your step," I said. "There's a lot of poop."

"Oh, I've been around chickens," she replied, stepping gingerly among the hens. I followed her in, and Duane followed me, looking around with an air of appraisal. Jeannie and I ventured through the coop and out the back door into the muddy run where I picked up chickens and held them out for her to pet.

"They're so soft, aren't they?" I said, caressing a brown hen's lofty back feathers. I showed her Bleach Blonde then Thunder Storm, one of our biggest birds with stunning black feathers. "Aren't her feathers so pretty?" I said. "They're iridescent in the sunlight."

Jeannie stood quietly gathering and murmuring over the chickens as I handed them to her. Then, I hunted around in the wood pile for the smaller of the two Polish hens and offered it to her. Jeannie held the small hen tucked tight against her wide chest as we talked in the drizzling rain and Duane stood framed by the coop door. I could see her love for the bird in the way she held it. It's such a gift to find someone who shares a love for the things you do.

"I thought they'd be all squawking around," her husband said.

"No, they're really calm," I replied.

Finally, Duane shifted and the moment passed. We piled out of the coop and I ran inside for a carton of eggs. We stood talking for a few more minutes by their car; then they left, and I went back inside.

After dinner that night, I noticed a bowl of leftover rice in the refrigerator and thought how happy the birds would be to have it – our hens love rice. I pulled the bowl out and carried it to the coop. I circled around on my way and paused to toss a fair share to the old hens. Then, I walked through the new coop and out into the run. I placed a handful on the woodpile where the Polish hens were hiding; then, I stood in the middle of the run tossing cold Basmati rice into the air like a guest at a wedding reception, and the hens rushed and dove at my feet.

I don't have to talk a lot to Jeannie to know she sees my heart and knows me well enough to guess at the things I need but may not voice. With her, I experience a sense of communion that exists beyond communication, a meeting of hearts over shared love and compassion.

For me, something similar is true with the chickens. We connect - my love and compassion for them and their gentle acceptance of me bridges the divide be-

tween us and, without even speaking a word, I know that I'm less alone in the world. This is what communion does – bridging a gap, bringing what is separate together even if it's only for the briefest of moments on a rainy afternoon or when the sun peeks out at the end of a long day.

# 8  POOP MATTERS

Early this morning, I let the old hens out to free-range and then headed over to the big coop. The new hens startled at my approach, surprised by my early arrival. Inside the coop, the Polish hens honked and squawked as they were chased from corner to corner by the shoving and pecking of the older hens. Sensing their distress, I grabbed them and tucked them into the dog crate for a respite with food and water.

Then, I piled in food for the big girls and opened the door to give them access to the run. While the

babies ate, I turned to the big blue Rubber Maid Bins their previous owner gave us to use as nesting boxes.

The heavy bins had large doors cut into the side, creating a cave-like space that, with the addition of a little straw, made a perfect place for laying eggs. Before we had gotten the new flock, we built nesting boxes of our own by turning plastic cat litter containers on their sides and attaching them to a plastic shelving unit. The owner, though, thought the hens would be happier in their own familiar boxes, so we brought them home and sat them awkwardly on top of the shelves where the boxes we built stood.

Unfortunately, that made the lids of the Rubber Maid bins the highest and most familiar area in the room. This led to the chickens deciding, by mutual consensus it seems, that it would be a good idea to sleep crowded together on top of the bins. All ten birds tried, every night, to squeeze into a tiny, two-by-three foot area rather than roosting on the two wooden bars and a lovely tree branch we so thoughtfully provided. If the chickens slept on the bars, like they're supposed to, then their poop – which they produce in large quantities all night long – would fall to the floor and land in the hay where it could be easily removed on a regular basis. But because our thoughtless chickens refused to comply, the Rubber Maid nesting boxes got covered every night with thick mounds, huge spi-

rals of poop swirled like soft serve ice cream. That left me working every couple of days or so to try to clean the lids.

This morning the lids were piled high with dung in shades of black, gray, brown and white, and I knew it was time to clean up. I pried the rubber lids off gingerly, desperately hoping they wouldn't suddenly pop loose and fling poop into my face. Then, I carried them, one at a time, behind the garage to the compost heap and whacked them against the pallet sides, creating a solid rubber-against-wood thwack that resonated in a satisfying way. There was still a wet layer of poop caked onto the lid, and I grabbed a stick from the ground to scrape it off. Up on the hill behind our house, construction workers hammered on a neighbor's huge addition, their hammer's echoes offering a counterbalance to the sound of chicken poop being whacked off rubber.

Yesterday, Sophia announced at dinner that her teacher had written a bad word on the chalkboard at school that day. She said her teacher was explaining the law that makes it illegal for parents to give their children humiliating names. Sophia mouthed the word's spelling across the table to her father and me. Her

eight-year-old brother was all eyes and ears, desperate to not miss out on this highly-provocative information.

The word was "shit," and before long Solomon caught on and just like that, after ten years of keeping them out, a bad word entered the house. I can think of worse words, though.

"Do you know what it means?" I asked Sophia.

She shook her head no.

"It's another word for poop," I said. "I don't know why she didn't just use a different word like," and here I stood and wrote on the chalkboard that hangs on our dining room wall, "what if you named your kid Poo Ped?" This got a good laugh from everyone at the table, even the four-year-old twins, who were otherwise left out of the bad word conversation.

Sophia turns ten tomorrow, marking ten years of motherhood for me, and motherhood, as anyone who's tried it knows, involves a lot of poop. This morning I remembered that, with Isaiah and Levi soon turning five, my days of dealing with poop could be pretty much over if I wanted. We're finally done with diapers, done with potty-training, and even accidents, they mostly take care of by themselves. So why, I wonder, did I bring in these shitty birds that tie me to refuse and feces, who crap when and where they want

throughout the yard or, as was the case last night, directly into the mouth of the Water Boy waterer?

It's possible I wasn't thinking about the fecal matter involved when I went after these birds. But we did already have two years of poultry experience, so one would suspect I was pretty aware of the fact that the only thing chickens make, other than eggs, is poop. Chickens are, in fact, particularly prodigious poopers.

But somehow I know that the messy reality of farm life was exactly what I was after when I decided to increase our flock four-fold.

A friend of mine gave a sermon recently about poop. Using a clip from the movie *The Martian* in which the stranded hero re-hydrates human feces to use as fertilizer for life-saving crops, my friend talked about the "stuff" of our lives that we deem irrelevant, un-useful. "God never wastes a mistake," he said. One woman at my table was deeply offended by the sermon on poop, almost as offended as I was with whichever bird pooped directly into the Water Boy's open mouth.

I think I get it, though. Life is messy. Anne Lamott says in her book, *Bird by Bird*, ". . . clutter and mess show us that life is being lived." Mess, or in this case, poop, can be a good sign of a healthy life. If we spend all of our time and energy trying to avoid a mess, we may well end up avoiding life as well.

But beyond that, what my preaching friend suggested is that fecal matter is more than just a signpost that life is happening. What he was suggesting is that poop, the by-product of the good stuff of life, has actual value in and of itself. This too applies to chickens – chicken dung is a great fertilizer, and every time we move the chicken tractor to a new patch of grass, we leave a rectangle of verdant green grass in its wake.

This idea is one I've spent a lot of time wrestling with as a parent, whether the hard parts, the messy parts, of life are just a necessary evil or whether they have actual value and meaning in and of themselves. I think my purchase of these birds indicates I'm leaning toward the latter.

This morning, I sat tucked into the corner of the loveseat cuddling our big, black tomcat, enjoying a few moments of welcome quiet before the boys exploded down the stairs. Sophia, curled at the other end of the couch, sat watching me. "I love my cats," I said, snuggling the cat against my chest, rubbing his ears and purring throat. "What kind of pets do you want to have when you grow up?" I asked.

"Cats," she said.

"How many?" I asked.

"Five or six," she said, "or eight."

I envisioned the litter boxes involved with that number of cats. I envisioned the poop. Did she know how much eight cats could poop? But then I remembered she regularly scoops out our own two litter boxes, and I realized she probably understands the implications better than I think.

"Anything else?" I asked.

"A dog, some gerbils," she said, listing the pets we already own.

"Gerbils, to feed to the cats?" I teased.

She rolled her eyes, smiled, and then added, "Maybe some chickens, too."

# 9 NIGHT GUARDIANS

Isaiah called out in the night, waking me from a deep sleep. It was 3:40 am and I woke in the middle of a dream in which I was pregnant and mildly in labor. I was sleeping so hard that I didn't even bother to find my glasses before stumbling down the hall to the room he shares with Levi.

I fixed the blanket on Isaiah's bed, then walked across the room to adjust Levi's blanket too, hoping to save myself another middle of the night trip. Legos and other scattered toys transformed their floor into a minefield for my sleepy, stumbling feet. "Night-night, Mommy. See you in the morning," Isaiah mumbled.

"Night-night," I sighed. Returning to my bedroom, I found it warm and humid, filled with the heavy stillness of midsummer heat. I cracked a window and slid back into bed.

Twenty minutes later, my husband and I were startled awake by the sounds of a feral battle rolling in through the open window. Our tomcat was outside for the night, and by the sound of it, he was scrapping with something near the Christmas tree outside our window. Heart-stopping screams and snarls, the sounds of wrestling, pierced by interludes of low growling electrified the night. John stumbled out of bed and headed outside in his boxers, carrying (I later learned) a 2x4. I turned on the bedroom light and rapped on the window, anxious not to wake the kids but hoping to interrupt the fighting below. I was frantic for our cat, desperate for him to avoid real harm.

When John turned on the outside light, the screams trailed off toward the neighbor's yard, and I lay down again, quietly listening to the tinkle of tags on our dog's collar as she and John searched the yard. Then, with my husband still outside, the cat slipped quietly into our room and headed straight for his food bowl. How he could go from fighting to eating was beyond me, but he started choking down food like he was half-starved. A few minutes later John returned

and turned off the light. "Where'd you find the cat?" I asked.

"I didn't," he said.

"He's inside, eating," I said.

"Well, I didn't find him." John replied. "I was worried because I thought maybe he was fighting with a fox. He must have snuck inside when I wasn't looking."

Several months ago one of our oldest hens had been snatched from her nightly roost in the pine tree and eaten. Since then we've worried about the presence of predators on our property – a fox or maybe a hawk – and once they find an easy food source, like chickens sleeping in a pine tree, it's guaranteed they'll return for more than one meal. The cat finally stopped eating and settled to sleep on the windowsill, still sniffing the cool night air. The adrenalin rush slowly receded, and I returned to a fitful sleep, dreaming of chickens escaping their run - auburn chickens and blondes, teeming in a pen and escaping to the roof and yard, a flock of chaos spreading in the night.

Morning brought heavy rain, and when I went to check on the new flock, I found most of them clustered inside the coop. I felt a familiar sense of dread, though, when I couldn't find the Polish hens. I walked out into the run and scanned the overgrown shrubs lining the wall of the garage and bent to peer into the

cave-like hole in the wood pile where they often hide. There weren't many places they could be, and my worry grew as I again scanned the empty run. Something had been in the yard last night, something fierce enough to challenge our big cat. Was it possible that whatever it was had run off with a Polish hen or two? Of course, it was possible. That's the thing with the dark cover of night. Night brings vulnerability and risk, too often placing us and the ones we love in danger.

I stood still in the run, wondering what I was missing and then I heard a distinctive peeping sound, like a chorus of tiny bicycle horns. Listening closely, I followed the noise to a corner where the blue plastic tarp covering the wood pile created a snug, dry overhang. I lifted the dripping tarp to reveal the Polish hens snuggled together, safe and dry.

Sophia, our oldest child, was born ten years ago today. Labor with her was long and confusing as my husband and I battled with the worry and uncertainty of first-time parents. We had vague ideas about labor based on books we'd read and a brief birthing class, but when early labor arrived, it was subtle and unclear. We waited through a night then went to the hospital only to be sent home disappointed. I cried as we left

the maternity ward and discouragement blossomed. Finally, after being in mild labor for nearly 24 hours, I took a sleeping pill my midwife had prescribed and went to bed. Several hours later, I woke to the feeling of a breeze brushing across my face. Then, a contraction stretched and squeezed its way across my abdomen. I realized real labor had finally arrived and that the breeze I felt was a bat circling our bedroom in the dark.

Bats were common, though unwelcome, night visitors at our old house. They often squeezed in through vents in the roof and slipped into our bedroom, entering via thin gaps around the doors to the attic crawl spaces.

"John! John! There's a bat," I said, yanking the covers over my head. Contractions bore down, and I scuttled out of the room with my head ducked, carefully closing the door behind me. John battled the bat while I waited next door in the empty nursery, anxious to leave for the hospital. John caught it in a laundry basket and released it outside before running back upstairs to get me and the overnight bag. We drove off into the night together, not knowing it would still be almost nine hours before we were out of the dark completely, before the vulnerability of new beginnings passed, and we held a little girl in our arms.

Last night's chaos reminded me of the night I labored with my daughter. The sense of vulnerability and danger, the relief of the cat's return and the house growing quiet again at last. Being woken to labor by a bat has always seemed like a potent symbol to me, but it's taken me ten years to look into it any further. This morning, on the day of Sophia's birthday, I checked on-line. Bats, it seems, are a symbol of death and rebirth.

Ten years ago my daughter, my first child, was born. Ten years ago, life as I knew it ended, and a new life was born. Google also reveals that bats are referred to as "Guardians of the Night." This is an image I like, a bat hovering in the night as we drift between spaces, between wakefulness and sleep, between one way of life and another. In times of transition, we all need a guardian of some sort or another, be it a bat, a cat, or a mother's cool hand tugging a blanket into place.

We don't get bats here in our new house, but we wake still in the night. We wake to tuck in our children and fetch a cup of water, to rescue the cat or a chicken if need be. We wake in the night to guard what we've been given, all that's been born as we

travel together through every long and short night toward morning.

# 10 OPEN HEART

Cold winds and thunderstorms settled into the area over the weekend. Saturday came and went in a fog of post-birthday-party exhaustion, and the sunny morning turned dark and windy by late afternoon. In the morning, our sleepy kids stayed inside playing on the Wii, and I walked down to the fence, hoping to talk awhile with our neighbor Ann.

I spotted her husband, Don, in the yard first, closer to the fence. Based on two years of over-the-fence observation, I've reached the conclusion that Ann and Don's yard is governed by a neat division of labor –

Ann tends her teaming flowerbeds and Don putters in his vegetable garden. Both the beds and the garden put ours to shame, but John and I comfort ourselves by remembering that the Ann and Don are retired and not raising four young children.

I've noticed a similar division of labor in their approach to the neighborly business of fence-side small-talk – Ann engages freely in extended conversation over a wide range of topics, and Don does not. Drawing Don to the fence to even ask a question is like pulling teeth. Attempt more and he's clearly uncomfortable.

One day last summer, when we were integrating our second round of chicks into our well established flock, the twins discovered one of the chicks named America, trapped tight in the far corner of the run. "She's dead! America's dead!" they cried, running into the house and pulling me out into the yard. Bending down to examine the chick I discovered a large bloody gash in her neck. It looked, in fact, like she'd been decapitated. I wasn't sure what to do, and, more importantly, I didn't want to deal with the dead bird alone while Isaiah and Levi ran enthusiastic circles around me.

Standing up, I looked down toward Ann and Don's yard hoping for help. I caught a glimpse of Don and approached casually under the guise of commiserating

but seriously hoping to convince him to take care of the dead bird. Don, however, proved resilient in the face of my woman-in-distress ploy.

"Oh," he said, "that's too bad." He didn't offer to help, and, knowing it wasn't his responsibility, I couldn't bring myself to ask. I would deal with the bird myself.

When I got back to the chicken tractor I bent down again for a closer examination. The twins, bored already with death, had wandered off and in their absence, I noticed the rise and fall the chick's fluffy feathers. She was still breathing, a clear sign she had not, in fact, been decapitated. I walked into the run and reached into the far back corner where she was huddled. Pulling her out and tucking her to my chest, I realized she was pecked up pretty badly but likely to survive. After a few days of isolation and over-the-counter antibiotic ointment, she was on the mend, and I had learned not to expect Don to play the Knight in Shining Armor.

So I wasn't looking to talk to Don Saturday morning, I was looking for Ann. I spotted her on the far side of their yard wearing shorts and tall black polka-dotted rain boots. Easily forgetting she's close to 70 years old, I watched as she pushed a wheelbarrow full of mulch around to her flower beds. Seeing my approach, she made a bee-line to the fence, and we chat-

ted about summer and the gigantic addition being added to a house on the hill behind our house. While we talked, Isaiah and Levi ran over yelling, "Miss. Ann! Miss. Ann!" They climbed briefly up and down the fence, lapping up her attention, then trotted off to play again.

The reason I walked down to the fence was that I needed someone to talk to. The night before John and I had found out that dear friends of ours were separating, and our hearts were broken. When our chit-chat wound down, I told Ann about it. She affirmed the real pain of a marriage ending and how sad it is for everyone involved, sharing stories from her experience with the divorces of people she knows.

So many of the married friends John and I share got married at the same time we did. We knew, even then, that the odds were high that many of us would not stay married. And yet now, some 15 years later, it still seemed impossible that some of our friends were entering into a post-marriage stage of life.

"Maybe we're naïve," I said, "I'm almost 40. I don't understand how these things still catch me by surprise." What I really couldn't understand was why it hurt so badly – hurt to see our friends in such complete and utter pain, hurt to be unable to fix it for them, to only be able to stand by watching, listening, and praying.

Turning back to face our yard, I noticed the Polish hens and asked Ann if she'd seen them. She said she had but couldn't really tell much about them since they were penned up in the run on the far side of our yard. "Do you see the fluff-headed ones?" I asked, my eyes following the Polish hens as they pecked along the perimeter of the netting.

"Yeah, kinda," she said, "but not very well."

I described them for her in detail, painting a picture of their fluffy white pom-pom heads and lacy gray-black feathers. As I talked, I felt love for them rise in my chest despite the distance between us.

Later in the day, I told John about my conversation with Ann, about how I thought maybe we were just naive. But I also told him something I had realized while standing at the fence watching those baby hens from a distance. "I loved them," I said, "even from all the way across the yard, and I guess if you're the kind of person who can fall in love with a Polish hen, then life's gonna hurt."

"What do you mean?" he asked.

"There's no separating the two," I said. "It's like the words on that painting hanging in the upstairs hallway, "Love wide; make your way with an open heart." Loving a Polish hen is loving with an open heart, and an open heart's gonna get hurt. But an

open heart also has access to the kind of joy that helps in the middle of the hurt."

Some days, I think that's the most we can hope for – enough joy to carry us through the hurt. Maybe also, if we're lucky, we might find a sturdy fence to lean on and a neighbor willing to listen for a few minutes or more.

# 11  FINDING HOME

Bleach-blonde continues to "fly the coop," and we can't figure out how she's escaping. Rain or shine, we find her wandering the driveway looking lost and confused but not alarmed. She accepts capture easily, sometimes walking right up to me as though she wants to be picked up. Her body language says, "I'm lost. Can you help me find my way back home?" Every time I gather her up she responds with a matter-of-fact sound, a low moan that rises from deep in her chest. "Yeah, I know," I say, mimicking her sounds as I carry her back to the coop.

John shuts the new hens into their coop every night now when he takes the dog out one last time before bed. After walking the dark yard with the dog, he counts the hens and, if all are accounted for, bolts the door tight. Last night, short one hen, he discovered Bleach-blonde perched on the wooden staircase that leads to the attic of the garage. The staircase begins by the coop door and runs along its one wall. It seems Bleach-blonde knows where the other chickens are but can't figure out how to get back into the run once she's out. Settling for proximity, she clambers up the wooden stairs and falls asleep there, separated from her flock by a wall.

The old flock has been a little lost lately, too. We recently started moving the chicken tractor after leaving it parked in one spot, sandwiched between the big and little houses, all winter long. Pulling it forward 10 to 12 feet every day or two gives the girls a new patch of ground to scratch and prevents them from destroying the grass in any one spot. Moving the tractor down into the yard, we turn it in one direction then another to avoid trees, bushes, and uneven terrain. Over the course of a week, it gets parked at different angles throughout the yard.

Recently, I noticed that turning the coop so the door faces east, say, rather than west thoroughly confuses the hens – they're unable to find the door. This

is both amusing and frustrating when trying to get them inside for the night. Reading online, I discovered chickens judge direction based on the earth's electro-magnetic field; in other words, they actually know north from south. Rather than memorizing the layout of their coop, they memorize what direction the door faces and continue to be surprised when it isn't there. It seems, when given a choice, chickens prefer their houses to stay in one place, and I have to say I agree.

I talked to my parents yesterday about their on-going search for a house. Both are retired and aging rapidly, and they've been talking for years about selling their home in northern New York and moving closer to either my brother or me. Their move has been long-delayed by on-going health issues, but yesterday, my mom called with the unexpected news that they put an offer on a house about 20 minutes from my brother in the Shenandoah Valley of VA.

I was surprised. In the past, they've wanted at least an acre of land, preferably in a wooded area. The house they were now considering was on a third of an acre in a suburban development. I asked my mom about their change of mind. She told me they simply couldn't find the kind of place they were originally looking for. They spotted one house with land but

soon heard from a realtor that the woman next door ran a pet shop and kept all kinds of animals at her house. "I don't want to be next to something like that," my mom said. "Anything we found with a little land in the country had a horse farm or a pig farm right next to it," she explained.

Later, walking out to tend to the chickens, I looked around our small farm with appraising eyes. It wasn't a functioning farm when we moved in two years ago, but it was when it was first built – a pig sty stood behind the garage, and the building that houses my office was originally a chicken coop. In two years, we've brought the place back toward a farm, tilling up the manicured lawn to add first two, then four, then six garden beds. With the gardens came pets – chickens first, then kittens and a dog – and John has high hopes for, someday, a goat. We installed a wood burning stove - to save on oil heat - and the yard has since filled with chopped and semi-chopped wood.

The pets and wood add chaos and mess, but even they're no match for the havoc wreaked by four kids. Broken tree limb forts covered in torn tarps dot the landscape while abandoned scooters and bikes litter the driveway. When they aren't climbing trees and hammering boards into them, they're digging holes faster than we can fill them. We brought the place back toward a farm and, in the process, added a lot of

chaos and mess. Farming is less picturesque than coffee table books, with their glossy images of the new suburban farmer, lead you to imagine. That's why farmers own things like work clothes and muck boots.

Next to our house, on a track of land subdivided from the original farm, sits a tidy little development of new homes. The yards are big, by development standards, immaculate, and rarely used. On the hill behind us, one of those homes is completing a magnificent addition that looks, from down here, a bit like a castle. Some days when I'm feeling self-conscious about our way of life, I imagine the people in those houses looking down on our wide open, mess-filled yard. "What are they doing?" the imaginary neighbors in my mind ask themselves. There aren't any chickens in those yards – in fact we recently found out neither chickens or chain link fences, both of which we have, are allowed within the development.

Looking around the driveway and yard after the conversation with my mom, I wondered whether we might be dragging down the real estate values in our neighborhood. A familiar feeling of dis-ease and shame about our way of life crept in. Walking into the house after a day of writing and tending the hens, I crossed the chaos of our mud room, like Moses and the Israelites crossing the Red Sea. Piles of shoes, coats, tools and projects – old and new – lined either side of my

path. I told my husband about the conversation with my mom as we prepped dinner in the kitchen that night. Did he feel shame about our way of life? Did the mess and chaos bother him too?

My mom grew up the daughter of a share-cropper in North Carolina. Her family was poor by any standards, and her father raised pigs and grew tobacco. Cleanliness was prized though difficult to attain and remains, all these years later, high on her list of priorities. I remember my mother saying of other women she didn't know well, "I don't know what kind of mother she is, but her kids are always clean." This was a bottom-line form of praise.

Meanwhile, over here on the farm, my kids are rarely clean, and my house is most often a terrible mess. If, as Anne Lamott says, "clutter and mess are a sign that life is being lived," one glance at our house and yard will tell you we're living a whole heck of a lot of life.

My husband and I were both raised in families that placed high priority on outward appearances. This is fine, to a point, but can be stifling, especially when life seems to be leading you in a different direction.

This is what I thought about as I passed through the mud room that afternoon – the reason we're able to endure the chaos and clutter is that we're being led in a different direction. Like those chickens orienting

according to the earth's electromagnetic field, my husband and I are trying, as best we can, to live in a way that honors the things behind the surface of our lives, and the results can be both frustrating and amusing.

That afternoon a thunder storm, one of the first of the summer, blew in. I woke from a nap on the loveseat to the noise of Isaiah and Levi trying to close the old roller blinds in the living room and thereby breaking them. The blinds were installed by the previous owner and were brittle and yellowed with age, but we left them hanging because they still mostly worked and new blinds are expensive.

"We're making it dark so we can see the lightening," they said, grinning with guilt when I woke and surveyed the damage.

"It's ok," I said, closing the last few blinds and joining them on the couch where we sat facing the window. Together, we watched the world turn up-side down as wind and rain whipped the tall, blue-green wheat growing in the field across the street.

Sometimes, I'm not sure whether we find home or home finds us, whether we really have a choice in the kind of life we live or whether it's something rooted in us that manifests itself in rooms and walls and yards tidy and untidy alike. What I do know is we all get

lost from time to time especially when life gets turned around by deaths and births and everything in-between. In those times, we might be wise to follow Bleach Blonde's example and look for a helpful stranger, someone who might gather us up with compassion and point us back in the right direction.

# 12  LOSS AND JOY

John and I sat together at the kitchen island this afternoon. I had just finished paying bills and balancing our checkbook, and it was time to fill him in on the finances. While I crunched numbers, he had been outside splitting wood with an axe, stacking it piece by piece to dry in the yard and keep down next winter's heating bills.

The money news was grim, as it most often is, and John was discouraged by the hours of seemingly endless work involved in burning wood. While the kids watched TV in the other room, we both slumped on our stools, taking a few moments to let a good bit of

accumulated stress and heartache ooze out in conversation.

As we talked ourselves deeper into a drought of discouragement and despair though, I kept being distracted by the sight of the Polish hens hunting and pecking outside the kitchen window. They were finally old enough to free-range along with the rest of the new flock, but those two stuck together in the yard, constantly bumping against each other and exchanging a strange chorus of sounds. Watching them, I felt a smile creep across my face.

"Look at those two," I said, interrupting our tirade of frustration and pointing out the window.

John smiled at the sight of them. "They're awesome," he said.

We both grew quiet then, watching the hens turn and march off, their stilt-like legs stepping in perfect time with each other, a little two-bird parade. Somehow our problems felt a little more manageable then or maybe just a little less consuming.

Later that night, after the kids were in bed, John ran out to the grocery store, and I went to the living room to pick up where I'd left off reading Frank McCourt's memoir, *Angela's Ashes*. Walking past the stairs toward the living room where I planned to curl up on

the couch, I felt the distinct weight of sadness in my chest. It sat on my left, just above my heart, in the place where you rest your right hand while saying the pledge of allegiance. To become aware of one's sadness is a significant thing; most of us spend a lot of time, energy, and money to avoid negative feelings. It's only in recent years that I've located the place in my body where sadness hides and I've learned to say its name not with fear, but with recognition, as though greeting an old friend.

It's not hard to dredge up a list of possible reasons for my sadness. I had pulled my back, straining my muscles yet again while trimming the hedges or stretching in yoga the day before. I can't say how much worse it will get before it gets better; all I can say is that I felt a twitch this afternoon and knew I was a goner. This last week of school is inherently stressful, and the open-ended chaos of summer looms on the horizon. Money's tight.

It's easy to make a list, but is it helpful? Who can say what roads sadness traveled to rest in my heart that night? Maybe it's enough to notice when it's arrived.

The living room was dark, and I switched on a small reading lamp in the corner. The open windows seem to expand and contract like lungs, breathing in a cool, evening breeze. I folded myself into the corner of

the couch. My floral, pajama pants comforted me with a calming bouquet of lavender and mauve.

*I'm sad,* I thought to myself with the closed book heavy in my hand. I felt the words tucked close to my heart like that shipping label on boxes that reads, "Fragile: Handle with Care."

*What do you do for sadness?* I wondered. No one answer came. I was still learning how to feel sadness and let it be, how to welcome it like a guest as the Sufi poet Rumi suggests. I was already well-practiced, though, in the old tricks of eating, drinking, and reading for comfort.

When John returned home, I knew he knew I was sad, but we didn't talk about it. He sat down on the other couch, looking at his phone, and I kept reading while licking salty pretzels and sipping his gin and tonic. When I knocked the glass over with an awkward reach, he jumped and ran for a towel, but I stayed put, making my way, page by page through McCourt's devastating life.

In the dark after we went to bed, I turned on my side and asked John to rub my lower back where the muscles were stretched taut like thick ropes hardpressed to hold everything in place. His fingers explored the topography of my back until he found a spot that burned like fire at his touch. "Ouch! Yes, that's the spot," I said. He pressed his thumb into the

pain as hard as he could, massaging the knot until his thumb grew weak.

I woke with every toss and turn that night, careful not to strain my back as I eased from side to side. We slept the whole night through wrapped around each other, bumping and nudging against each other as we shifted and turned, seeking the comfort closeness brings. Even the Polish hens know to do that much.

In the morning, I knew this is what you do for sadness: When sadness has had its say, you encourage it to look out the window and take heart at some small wonder in the yard. You wear it on your chest and feel it in your back. You read it stories from a book and allow someone you love to press into it with their thumbs. You wrap yourself around what comfort you can find, and in the morning, the birds and the kids and the sun will all be there again, and you will be ready to see them for the joy they are.

# 13  ALL SHALL BE WELL

We were late leaving for the twins' pre-school graduation program last night. I had harbored a growing anxiety about the event in the days and weeks leading up to it. It was scheduled for late in the evening on a school night, and we all needed to be dressed up, the twins especially. The mere logistics of getting six people dressed up and out the door on time on a school night were enough to cause panic. Beyond that, though, lay the emotional demands of the evening.

Preschool graduation is a rite of passage in our culture, and the graduation of your youngest offspring

marks the end of a parenting era – this was not only preschool graduation, but the *last* of our preschool graduations. Such occasions demand photographs – lots of them – and feelings. My fear wasn't that I would become overly emotional, smearing my non-existent mascara, but that I would somehow fail to significantly honor the emotional weight of the occasion.

John and I tend to go low-key at these events. We don't run down the aisle to take pictures; we don't stand at the back the whole time bobbing and weaving with a video camera in hand. We try to be present as best we can, but when so many people around you are behaving otherwise, it can begin to feel like you're under-valuing The Most Important Moment of Your Life.

I was already losing my babies; I didn't want to lose whatever emotional response I was expected to have. What if we didn't take enough pictures? Could I live with the regret? What if I didn't cry enough or laugh enough or whatever combination of the two the moment demanded? What if I failed to memorize the sound of their little voices on stage, the sweetness of their faces, the weight of their bodies in my arms after the show? I feared my own inadequacy times two.

That night, I hid my anxiety behind a wall of frustration which grew as the evening progressed. The twins wore matching button down shirts and khaki

pants. This itself was a feat of maternal organization, and I should have paused for a moment of satisfaction, but I didn't think the rest of us were dressed up enough, and beyond that, we were running late.

Once we piled out the door, I grabbed the keys from my poor husband and threw myself into the driver's seat of the van. I made it clear, both with words and without, that he was moving too slowly to get us there on time. But as soon as I started the van, my oldest son popped out of his seat and ran into the house to get something he'd forgotten. What could possibly be so important was completely beyond me, but I couldn't very well drive off with him inside, so I waited. Minutes later, I watched as he ran out in mismatched socks and worn-out shorts, leaving the back door wide open in his wake.

Someone would have to go back and close the doors, but I needed to move now. As soon as he was back in the van, I threw it into reverse, aiming to turn around and pull out of the driveway. The kids, excited and nervous and oddly invigorated by my own obvious frustration, bounced and jabbered in the back of the van like monkeys at the zoo. As I reversed, John started yelling, "Van! Van! Van!" It wasn't until I felt the van's bumper slam into the side of his truck that I realized what he meant to say was "Truck! Truck! Truck!"

A stunned silence settled over the van.

"Do you want me to drive?" John asked without skipping a beat.

All I could hear was the insinuation in his offer, the unspoken accusation that I was a little too unhinged to be driving. I gave him the dirtiest look I could muster and jumped out of the driver's seat, slamming the door behind me as hard as I possibly could. I ran back into the house, through the two doors my oldest son had left wide open, and stopped in front of the medicine cabinet. I pulled out the little red pill bottle and took the half anxiety pill I should have taken earlier. Then I shut the doors and walked out to the van.

I decided to let my husband drive.

We arrived in time after all, and much to my relief, we were less dressed up than some but more dressed up than others. I had even remembered to grab the teacher appreciation gifts. Maybe it was the medicine taking effect, but it seemed like we were going to be ok.

We dropped the twins off with their teachers then stood in the lobby considering our seating options. I had overheard parents asking the teachers which side of the stage their child would be on so they could be sure to sit in a corresponding section of the audience thus ensuring The Best Possible View of their child. Not wanting to be negligent, I scurried over and asked,

too. After glancing at the program, the teacher smiled, "They're on opposite sides," she said. "Maybe just try sitting in the middle."

We filed into the middle section, back row. The show started late, leaving plenty of time to peruse the printed program and note what each graduate wants to be when they grow up. I was delighted to discover I'm raising an artist and an officer of the law. Finally, the preschoolers filed on stage, and the twins were in the front row on opposite sides of the stage. My eyes ping-ponged between them throughout the program. Isaiah was doughy and sweet and oh so tired, his face melting into giant yawns at regular intervals. Levi was determined and focused, nailing the songs and hand motions.

After singing, the children sat in a row along the edge of the risers, and each walked alone to a microphone to say their name and what they like best about preschool. They had practiced with the microphone at school, so we were prepared for what was coming. I had told the twins I would pay them $5 each if they would say, "My favorite part of preschool is tooting!" They both were outraged at my suggestion. Clearly, in their opinion, preschool graduation was no laughing matter.

I felt my heart lurch when it was Levi's turn to speak. He struggles with speech, and I worried he'd

get stuck or freeze, but fear turned to relief as he spoke quickly into the microphone and rushed back to his seat. Several more students went, including one girl who froze in fear before delivering her sentence, before we got to Isaiah's turn.

Preschool programs are sweet, but with 20 or more students involved, they can get long, especially when the only child you're really there to see is your own. Waiting for Isaiah's turn, though, I felt lucky to have not one but two boys up on the stage. The arrival of twins brought a sense of abundance that began with a surprising ultrasound five years ago and continues to reverberate through our lives. Although at first it frightened me to no end, I don't know if I will ever stop being surprised to find myself gifted with not one but two extra boys in my life. Now that the fear has faded, the abundance itself is a continual source of gratitude.

After the program, we collected Isaiah and Levi and filed out to the foyer, where another parent offered to take a group picture of us. John said yes before I could say no, and we were captured in the camera frame, tired and happy, not-dressed-up-enough and late, but together still at the end of the night.

Out behind the school, volunteers served up dishes of Italian ice, and all three boys ran up and down a steep grassy hill, using the sugary blue slush as fuel.

They ran up and stood silhouetted against the sky, before plunging down, weaving like slalom skiers and narrowly missing children running in the opposite direction. The beauty of the moment was paired with constant fear of collision. When they were thoroughly worn out, we piled back into the van and drove home in the fading evening light.

John ushered the kids inside to start the bedtime routine; and I ran out to lock the older hens in for the night, hoping to find a moment of quiet after the evening's events. I grabbed a handful of cereal from the kitchen and approached the chicken tractor. One, two, three hens popped out and scuttled down the plank. But where was the fourth hen, America?

I shut the door to the run to prevent the three already inside from escaping. Then, I looked toward the Christmas tree and called, thinking maybe she was roosting there. Nothing moved in the tree. Walking closer, I scanned the branches. Finding it empty, I returned to the chicken tractor and circled around to the back. I opened the nesting box and peered into the coop and found, again, no sign of America. I started to feel a certain dread – a missing chicken is most often a dead chicken.

Moving back to the front of the tractor, I looked down at the hen's feeder, which had somehow toppled over onto its side. I hadn't noticed it before. Earlier

in the day I had watched, from a distance, as one of the hens stood on the edge of it eating from the top rather than from the small rim where food is distributed. Now the feeder lay on its side. Looking closer, I noticed a chicken butt sticking out of the feeder's open end. America's brown, gray and auburn tail feathers lay perfectly still. There was no sound, no movement. She must have died, I thought, the feeder tipped over with her in it and she died while struggling to get out.

Frustrated, I leaned over to take a closer look. Then, I saw her face, her burnt sienna beak and her blinking orange eye which stared back at me as if asking, "Are you going to get me out of here or what?" She was very much not dead.

I picked up the bucket and tugged her out backward, wrangling the handle out of the way of her backside. I had to pull pretty hard to get her loose, but she jumped out of my hands the second she was out and ruffled her feathers as if to shake off the indignity.

Most things, it seems, come out all right in the end, even if you have to endure a few bumps and dents along the way.

# 14  BETTER TOGETHER

Yesterday we put away the dog crate we used to separate the Polish hens from the rest of the flock, and now they're fully immersed in the new coop with the adult hens. They still keep to themselves, bumping along beside each other in nearly constant physical contact and whenever they're separated they peep and honk back and forth in a kind of call and response until they find each other again.

I read recently that the bouffant of feathers on the top of their heads, which earn ours the nick-name "Fluff-heads," renders them the chicken's equivalent of legally blind. Being legally blind, as a chicken, has the

unfortunate consequence of making one easy prey. Polish hens' vulnerability produces an uncommonly skittish and docile breed and helps me to understand their bumping together, which may well be the chicken's equivalent of holding hands.

Today, for the first time ever, we collected 12 eggs – a solid dozen. I'd be more excited about it if we didn't already have four dozen in the refrigerator. Production, you see, is outweighing demand. So far we've sold eggs to friends via word of mouth and online posts, but with production this high, we need to reach a wider market. I foresaw this problem and planned to hang a wooden sign along the busy road in front of our house, possibly even eventually adding a farm stand, but like most non-emergency projects around our house, the sign was long-delayed.

The sign was slated to be a collaborative project as I needed John to design, build, and hang the sign and I planned to paint it. In the weeks following the new chickens' arrival, we had several unfruitful discussions about the project. "We have too many eggs," I would lament, standing in front of the open refrigerator. "I need you to make a sign."

"What kind of sign do you want?" he would ask.

"Just a sign," I would reply, "a sign to hang by the side of the road."

"But I don't know what you want," he would say. Then, the topic would be dropped as indecision collided with some other more pressing matter like cooking or mowing or any of a hundred other tasks immediately at hand. Days would pass, sometimes a week; then, I would again stand in front of an egg-filled refrigerator, and the conversation would begin again.

One Saturday, though, while the kids were absorbed in electronics, we found enough space to stop mid-conversation-loop and walk out to the wood shop together. John rounded up a few old boards and laid them out side-by-side on his work bench. "Is this what you want?" he asked. It wasn't exactly what I was thinking, but we jiggered the boards around a little, added another, and I was satisfied. I went back to washing breakfast dishes while he figured out how to attach the boards together. Then it was my turn in the garage to finish the sign.

I layered the old boards with several coats of white paint, then penciled in the outline of plump hen and the words "Fresh Eggs," using what I hoped looked like a vintage-style farm font. We had an open quart of raspberry red paint left-over from painting the chicken tractor, and once the white paint dried, I car-

ried the sign in to the kitchen island to work on filling in the image and lettering.

It was slow work. Maybe I had the wrong kind of brush, but the paint went on thin and needed to be layered several times, slowly and carefully, before it looked right. I finished the chicken and three or four of the letters before it was time to make dinner. Then, I tucked the nearly-finished sign in a corner of the kitchen where it's stayed ever since.

So getting back to matter of the four dozen eggs in our refrigerator, I guess I need to finish that sign, pronto. I've been busy, yes, but there's something else holding me back. Namely, if we put out a sign, people will see it and know what we're doing. That's what advertising does, right? But something about putting ourselves (and our wares) out along the side of the road for all to see feels a little risky, maybe something like walking around with a big fluff of feathers on the top of your head. The Polish hens are amazing, but they sure don't blend-in and their uniqueness makes them vulnerable.

After a lot of delays (see previously mentioned approach to non-urgent situations), paperwork, and testing, the twins are starting speech therapy this summer. Earlier this week, we drove a town over to an elemen-

tary school where I thought we were set to begin therapy. But when we arrived there it became clear that we were only there to meet the therapist and fill out yet another round of paperwork. After months of waiting, it was a bit anticlimactic. We were disappointed. I steered the van halfheartedly toward home, cutting through a cold, gray rain. Halfway home, I remembered we were on course to pass right by Ashcombe Farm and Greenhouse.

Although the greenhouse is in decline and the gift shop overpriced, Ashcombe has been a winter destination for me ever since having kids. When the snowy ice and long, dark days of February set in and my longing for the sun and warmth of spring grows unbearable, I pack the kids into the van and drive the 15 minutes to Ashcombe.

Once there, we wander in the bright, humid greenhouse, absorbing the calm stillness of quietly breathing plants. A small fish pond gurgles among the plants, and two giant lop-eared bunnies live, caged, in a far back corner; a glass-walled beehive allows us to witness the slow production of golden sweetness.

Aside from room to walk and wonders to explore, Ashcombe also boasts a small café with simple, inexpensive lunches. The timing of the morning's botched speech appointment meant I would get home right at lunch time with two very hungry kids in tow. Re-

membering Ashecombe's café gave me an idea – maybe
a quick lunch out was exactly what was needed to re-
boot the day. I envisioned a warm bowl of soup for
me and hot dogs for the twins and steered the van toward both.

Once there, we made the requisite visit to the
greenhouse first, inspecting the goldfish and rabbits. I
lifted the twins one by one to watch the busy bees
working in the hive. We were hungry, though, so it
wasn't long before we headed inside to the café.
Aschombe is one of a few local places that offers
homemade food in a kid-friendly environment. Food is
served in a cafeteria style line then carried on lunch-
trays to a small, country-style dining area. Serving
homemade soups and sandwiches, it's a hit with the
older population which, for me, is one of the perks of
bringing my kids there for lunch. In my experience,
elderly people who are slowly eating a meal love
watching little kids, and I love watching them enjoy
the twins. I feel a sense of pride at their delight like a
mother hen parading her new chicks through a barn-
yard.

The day we stopped in for lunch was no exception;
the place was filled with elderly couples eating their
quiet meals and adult children lunching with their aging parents. The boys and I bought our food and settled at a wooden table of their choosing, me with a

bowl of tomato vegetable soup and the boys with plain hot dogs sitting in white paper wrappers. Levi was very impressed with the white wrappers.

I sat on one side of the table with steam from my Styrofoam bowl rising gently in front of me, and the twins sat across from me, side-by-side. Despite being seated, they stayed in constant motion, bumping and twitching, reaching and grabbing, as I filled precarious paper cups with pink lemonade and doled out potato chips.

The whole meal was a whir of motion and chatter. I was grateful for the wooden table that kept me separated from their swirling nucleus of energy, and I battled chaos by strategically-adjusting cups and napkins away from flying elbows and forearms. Elderly men and women gazed at the boys, offering shy smiles of appreciation. I watched Isaiah and Levi invading each other's space with such ease and regularity, and I was reminded of the Polish hens, the way they bump and tussle along together, side-by-side.

The twins have always shared this intense physicality, riding together first in the womb then in the double jogging stroller and now preferring to ride together on one bike instead of two. There's a sureness that comes of being born into a premade community, I see the way it breeds confidence and ease in those two. Together, they're naturally resilient in the face of risk

and vulnerability; whether it be in the form of starting a new school or climbing to new heights in a favorite tree.

There's a lesson for me in the companionship of the twins and the Polish hens, the way they instinctively lean on each other. Maybe that's what I need, too, not just in the adventure and risk of small-scale chicken farming but also in the months of transition coming in the fall.

Later in the week, I messaged a farming friend online. "We're having a hard time selling eggs," I wrote.

"Yeah," she replied, "I've found people buy less if they have to actually interact with you to buy them. They're more likely to buy if they can just stop by and grab them whenever they want. Hang in there; it'll get better."

She's right, I know. But I needed to hear it from someone else, so I reached out via the web and bumped into her and she bumped back and I felt a little less alone, a little less vulnerable to my own fears and expectation. I felt better, and I set to work finishing the sign, and we hung it out by the road. Then, John and I started working on plans for a farm stand, where we can leave eggs and produce out for sale, like my friend suggested. The whole time I continued to

check in with my friend and her presence, her willing-
ness to be with me in this new adventure, was enough
to give me the confidence to continue bumping along
one step at a time.

.

# 15   HIDDEN TREASURE

O ur giant black chicken stood outside the open kitchen window clucking with vigor yesterday afternoon. Despite the high heat and humidity, she marched back and forth in the green grass, busily squawking with an air of self-importance, a clear sign she'd just laid an egg. "A-ha!" I thought. I knew the hens were hiding eggs somewhere because the day before I had only found four eggs in the nesting boxes. Frustrated, I had walked slow, searching circles around the yard, hunting for their secret nest.

Our 16 hens have a total of seven nesting boxes spread between two coops and one "alternative" nest

tucked in a pile of hay on the garage floor. They have plenty of good places to lay their eggs. But once every month or so, one hen establishes a new nest, and the other hens, no longer satisfied with the old nests, are quick to follow.

The first secret nest we found was tucked under a piece of plywood that had been abandoned at the base of our largest pine tree. In the sheltering shade of the old wood, resting in a shallow depression between two roots, lay a clutch of eighteen eggs. Since then, we've found clutches on wooden shelves in my husband's wood shop, in dark corners of the garage, and in the middle of a much-trampled flowerbed. The nests are cleverly hidden and nearly impossible to find despite hens sitting in them and coming and going back and forth from them during the day.

When I suspect the hens are hoarding eggs, I prowl the yard looking around the bases of shrubs and trees, I roam the garage looking for secret corners and shadowed shelves. Most importantly, I start paying attention to the chatter among the birds.

Every chicken we have, save perhaps for the shy Polish hen, announces her own freshly laid egg with a puffed chest and wide-spread wings, her beak opening to pronounce her pride with a voluminous round of "bawk-bawk-bigawk." This announcement can go on for a good five or ten minutes as the hen boasts and

celebrates her success. If I'm paying attention, I notice this cackle of delight and quickly head toward the loud-mouth, hoping to catch her coming or going from the secret nest.

That's what I did yesterday when I heard the black hen clucking up a storm right outside the kitchen window. I ran outside before she finished singing and explored the weedy flowerbed nearby, pushing aside leggy Cone Flowers and Daisy stems that refuse to yield more buds. I also looked at the base of the shrubs that need trimming, but still the nest evaded me. Lately, I'd noticed the hens hanging out around the old well-house that stands near the kitchen window, but I'd already checked the ancient trellis there with its climbing vines and knew, just knew, there wasn't anything there.

Still, I paused and scanned low again while the black hen with her feathers that shimmer iridescent blue and green chattered on behind me. Then my eyes caught it, just a glimpse of brown tucked in below the trellis, behind winding vines hidden in shadow. Kneeling, I gently pulled back the vines to reveal a sheepish brown hen who leapt up upon my intrusion and tottered off into the yard, clucking the song of a successful hen. Nestled in a cave of vines sat a pile of eggs, treasure revealed.

I turned and ran inside, clucking louder than any hen, to tell the kids to pause Netflix long enough to come admire the secret nest. Back outside, we counted, one-by-one, the brown, white, and blue eggs I pulled out of their secret shade. "Eleven eggs!" we shouted, elated with our success.

The kids ran back to the TV while I ferried the eggs inside in the upturned hem of my shirt. In the kitchen I eased the eggs gently onto the counter and sent my husband a text, "I found the secret nest!" I washed the eggs, checked for freshness, and put each into its own place in a new carton. Then, I slid the carton into the cool, dark shade of the refrigerator.

I don't know why the hens change their laying habits, why they refuse to utilize the seven perfectly-good nesting boxes they have, but I suppose it has something to do with predators and ancient longings they could not quite articulate even if they possessed the gift of human language. I want those eggs, though, as much as any fox or raccoon in the wild might because they're of value to me, and since I feed and shelter the birds (as much as they're willing to comply) I feel entitled, you might say, to certain benefits.

In light of our give and take arrangement, it's tempting for me to read nefarious motives into the

hens' habits. But whatever their reasoning may be, the chickens keep providing me with opportunities to experience the joys of hide and seek. The more I play, the more I learn about chickens, about myself, and about new ways of sniffing out hidden gems.

I've never found a hidden nest by shaming a bird. I've never sat a chicken down and had a stern talk eye-to-eye and told them they really should be more compliant, but I'd bet my money it wouldn't work. Now though, when I find myself looking to find where hidden treasure lies, I pay attention and listen close, then I follow the song of joy.

# 16  SUMMER VACATION

"This isn't the best summer ever," Solomon said through streaming tears. We were less than five hours into summer vacation when he made his pronouncement at the dinner table. My husband and I exchanged looks of frustration. But I have to say, for as much as that kid can frustrate me, we are so very similar.

I was ready to be done with the chickens today. They're laying eggs in a pile of extra hay we were saving outside the coop. Using their feet and plump

breasts, they carved out two perfect nests right there on the ground where the dog can help herself to eggs any time she wants. Apparently they're too lazy or too confused to use any of the seven nesting boxes provided.

One of the new brown hens continues, to my persistent mortification, to end up in the preschool playground next door. I saw her there this morning and tried luring her to the fence with a handful of cereal. She came at my call and peered eagerly at the treats I held in my outstretched hand, but I couldn't get her to scoot under the fence.

Later, working in the laundry room, I heard the sound of our neighbor's voice drifting through our open back door. "Heeeeyyyyy, heeeeeeyyyy," she called, long and lazy. Around her legs, preschooler voices echoed, "Heeeeyyyyy. Heeeeeyyyyy." I left my mountain of laundry and trotted out the back door. There, I saw her leaning out of the door to the school, surrounded by a flock of kids. "Your chicken's in the yard," she called.

I felt so foolish, so irresponsible, so annoyed. By the time I made my way out to where the hen was hanging out another teacher had already chased her back over the fence. *I can't control the chickens*, I thought. T*hat's the problem. And I can't climb that damn fence to bring them back every day, three times*

*a day either.* But there's more. Based on the six dozen cartons of eggs currently crowding our refrigerator, egg sales are down, way, way down. *What's the point,* I wondered, *if I can't even sell the freaking eggs?* I started to think like my son – this wasn't the best idea ever.

I couldn't control the kids, either, when they got home from their last day of school. The end of the year excitement left them worn and frazzled. The twins and I waited for the older kids on the sunny porch with happy summer smiles, but joy gave way to exhaustion by the time we got inside. Soon the Sophia and Solomon were snapping and snarling with each other. Isaiah and Levi, awake since six in the morning, only added to the chaos, whizzing around the room like lit firecrackers, igniting frustration and dispute wherever they landed. Things were bad enough that I played the biggest card in my hand, threatening to cancel our annual last-day-of-school ice cream trip if attitudes didn't improve.

We did make it out for ice cream, though, even after the tearful dinner. I remembered to remind the kids, who nearly froze at the year before, to bring their coats and they did with only a minimal amount of pushback. Properly protected against the cold, every-

one sat in their own chairs rather than climbing on John and I for warmth. Eating ice cream with two four-year-olds climbing on you is not enjoyable. This year, the cones were smaller and more manageable and, to my great amazement, we hardly need a single napkin.

We all sat around a tiny table in the neon yellow and midnight blue shop with checkerboard floor. Licking his cone contemplatively, Solomon asked, "Who's smarter, Daddy or Mommy?" Then the twins chimed in too, querying in their little lisping voices, "Who's farter?" We laughed, enjoying the sweetness on our lips and tongues. While the kids focused on their cones, John and I whispered back and forth about the impossibly-young boys manning the cash register.

"Are they twelve or what?" I asked under my breath.

"I can't imagine the one's old enough to drive," he said. "But maybe the other one could be 16." Then, after a pause, he added, "How can 16 even be old enough to drive?"

Sophia's too young yet to notice these sweet-faced, handsome boys. But I know one day soon she will, and sitting with her Dad, her brothers, and I will be completely devastating to her fragile teenage ego. Before long she'll be off and driving, running some ice cream parlor all on her own. Observing those boys at

the counter helped me see the little faces around our table in a different light. I found myself grateful for the sweetness of the moment, more tolerant of the accompanying chaos.

Maybe it won't be the worst summer ever.

Later, tucking the old flock into their coop for the night, I thought wistfully about how tidy and manageable a flock of four feels when compared to the adventure we began at the end of April. John put the kids to bed, and I mowed grass for almost two hours as the sky ripened around me like a peach. The cool evening air gave me goosebumps as I turned in smaller and smaller squares, cutting the last bits of grass in the middle of the yard.

While driving I pondered our problems – the hens, the kids, the endless mowing demanded by the summer months. I tried to wrestle each problem into a tidy answer, but I knew it was a no use. No matter how hard I work to organize the summer, to file the kids and I, the hens, into something I can control, it will inevitably overflow again into chaos. "*Maybe,*" I thought to myself, "*that's not such a bad thing after all.*"

# AFTERWARD

The Fresh Eggs sign is still out in front of the house and I still venture out on a daily basis, hunting for the eggs our hens hide in secret nests all around the yard and garage. Summer vacation is here in full, and my older kids have taken over the chicken chores.

Not long ago, we started to wonder about the gender of one the Polish hens whose wattle – the wobbly, red patch of skin that dangles from a chicken's neck – was growing in quickly and in a brilliant shade of red. We also noticed the beginnings of a comb – the bright red strip of flesh that grows on a rooster's head. Most hens have smaller wattles and combs that take a while

to make an appearance and the other Polish hen had yet to develop either.

We researched a little online but didn't reach a definitive conclusion until the hen in question started emitting sharp little cries at odd times of the day. The noise sounded painful to make and rose at the end like a question, "Errrrr?" I heard it first one morning and mentioned it to the kids. I thought maybe it was yet another part of Polish hen vernacular. But then we all started hearing it more and more often. Finally, we admitted, with no small sense of dread, that we had another rooster on hand. Given what happened to our previous rooster, the future didn't look terribly bright for the "hen" now known as Joker.

Joker, now sexually mature, is a bit of a dud as far as stereotypical roosters go, which works just fine for us and bodes well for his chances of remaining here on the farm. Roosters are typically aggressive toward hens and humans and often grow quite large, making them a truly intimidating presence. One friend I know has a rooster who stands over two feet tall, and she doesn't dare enter his run without a stick or some other means of protection. Joker isn't much bigger than our girls and still spends most of the day roaming the yard with his little fluff-headed companion.

But now, in early morning and evenings, he chases the hens, eager to sow his wild oats. As awkward as a

teenager growing his first mustache, he's not terribly fast and lacks the machismo typically seen in the males of his species. When he does manage to tackle one of the slower hens, he climbs about on her back and head, appearing uncertain about exactly how one approaches the business of mating. The hens sense his timidity and chase him off if he comes too close. He has started crowing more, but his "cock-a-doodle-doos" are missing a few of the traditional notes and end up sounding something more like a strangled "Ya-hoo!"

New neighbors moved into the development behind us recently. Their yard backs up along our fence line and after a long, full summer day the six of us trundled over to meet them. I checked for clean faces but left the kids in their sweaty clothes. Around the fence and up into the development we went with Isaiah carrying a bag of treats.

The bag held a jar of homemade strawberry jam and a batch of oatmeal cookie bars wrapped in parchment paper, both tied with lime green ribbons. The effect was surprisingly Martha Stewart for being utterly improvised, and I was proud of myself for pulling it together. John and the kids really wanted to take along a carton of eggs, but I didn't want to come across as being too "Farmer Brown."

We awkwardly stumbled across the neighbor and her three kids on the sidewalk before actually reaching their house, so we went ahead and introduced ourselves and handed over the goody bag. The topic of chickens came up in the mix of the "where are you from" and "how old are your kids" pleasantries.

"So you guys have chickens?" she asked.

"Yes," I said.

"Yeah," she said, "we've found them in our yard."

"Oh," my husband said, "sorry about that."

"No, that's fine," she said. "My daughter loves them. But we have a German Shepherd, he's ancient, but I'm pretty sure he will eat a chicken if he sees one."

We brushed it off as no big deal. Like I've said before, things happen to chickens. But inside I felt the familiar embarrassment at our inability to keep our birds in line.

Noticing a pause in the conversation, my oldest son spoke up with great enthusiasm. "We have a rooster," he said. "He's trying to mate! Joker used to be a girl, but now he's not. Now he chases the hens and sits on their heads because he doesn't exactly know what he's doing!"

John and I glanced at each other. We were both red in the face and eager to put an end to the mating conversation. The truth is our kids aren't exactly sure

what Joker's supposed to be doing either, and I didn't want to end up giving a full-blown sex talk right there on the sidewalk with our new neighbors looking on. I deftly steered the conversation to another topic, and soon our parade of six was hopping and skipping back down the hill toward home. We did eventually seal up all the holes in our fence, and their old, but gigantic, German Shepherd has yet to enjoy any of our chickens for dinner.

This is how we are, I think, how I am. I'm every bit as awkward as that rooster announcing himself to the world with a half-baked crow, one minute perched on the top of the wood pile, flapping his wings and singing with his chest puffed out, the next minute being cowed by the very hens he's supposed to protect.

Like him, I find myself teetering between who I am and who I'm becoming as I move toward discovering my own voice, my own way of being in the world. Most often I end up getting things awkwardly out of sorts. I'm proud of our chickens, our life, and the love it breeds, but I'm embarrassed, too, at times, at the mess and earthiness of it all. I'm not sure whether that will ever go away.

Recently, Isaiah approached while I washed dishes at the kitchen sink. Touching my leg to get my atten-

tion, he gazed up at me with wide brown eyes, "We're getting chicks soon, right?!" he asked. "The lady's going to give us chicks?"

"Yes," I said, "soon." He danced away, happy.

That's right, we're adding another four to our flock and, God help us, it's possible one or two will turn out to be a rooster. I don't know what we'll do if that happens. It's bound to be a mess, but that's what happens when you step out into life. Things get complicated, chaos blooms, and yet somehow, hidden right in the middle of the dirt and poop and brokenness are all the little treasures we covet most, like beauty, joy and love.

This is what it means to me to be a witness in the way the Psalmists and other biblical figures were, to learn to look at our lives I such a way that we begin to see the threads of mercy that run through every moment of every day. If we can learn to live this way, then every risk has its own rewards regardless of success or failure. Then we, like Joker and the hens and every child who ever was, won't be able to help but puff out our chests, raise our voices, and sing our delight at the beauty of all that is.

.

# ABOUT THE AUTHOR

Kelly Chripczuk is a licensed pastor, spiritual director and writer who lives in Central PA with her husband and four children. Their 110 year old farm house is also currently home to 18 chickens, two cats, one dog, a Siamese fighting fish, and a Parakeet. She writes regularly at her blog afieldofwildflowers.blogspot.com and offers occasional workshops and retreats. More information about upcoming events or scheduling an event can be found on her website.

Made in the USA
Middletown, DE
13 November 2016